Fresh Ways
with Soups & Stews

Time-Life Books Inc.
is a wholly owned subsidiary of
TIME INCORPORATED

FOUNDER: Henry R. Luce 1898-1967

Editor-in-Chief: Henry Anatole Grunwald
President: J. Richard Munro
Chairman of the Board: Ralph P. Davidson
Corporate Editor: Ray Cave
Group Vice President, Books: Reginald K. Brack Jr.
Vice President, Books: George Artandi

COVER
Meatballs of veal and sage are the counterpoint to a thin veal broth threaded with angel-hair pasta. The recipe for this soup, which contains a mere 240 calories per serving, is on page 56.

TIME-LIFE BOOKS INC.

EDITOR: George Constable
Director of Design: Louis Klein
Director of Editorial Resources: Phyllis K. Wise
Acting Text Director: Ellen Phillips
Editorial Board: Russell B. Adams Jr., Dale M. Brown, Roberta Conlan, Thomas H. Flaherty, Donia Ann Steele, Rosalind Stubenberg, Kit van Tulleken, Henry Woodhead
Director of Photography and Research: John Conrad Weiser

PRESIDENT: Reginald K. Brack Jr.
Executive Vice Presidents: John M. Fahey Jr., Christopher T. Linen
Senior Vice Presidents: James L. Mercer, Leopoldo Toralballa
Vice Presidents: Stephen L. Bair, Ralph J. Cuomo, Juanita T. James, Hallett Johnson III, Robert H. Smith, Paul R. Stewart
Director of Production Services: Robert J. Passantino

Editorial Operations
Copy Chief: Diane Ullius
Editorial Operations: Caroline A. Boubin (manager)
Production: Celia Beattie
Quality Control: James J. Cox (director)
Library: Louise D. Forstall

Correspondents: Elisabeth Kraemer-Singh (Bonn); Maria Vincenza Aloisi, Josephine du Brusle (Paris); Ann Natanson (Rome).

Library of Congress Cataloguing in Publication Data
Main entry under title:
Fresh ways with soups & stews.
(Healthy home cooking)
Includes index.
1. Soups. 2. Stews. I. Time-Life Books.
II. Series.
TX757.F74 1986   641.8'13   86-5883
ISBN 0-8094-5820-9
ISBN 0-8094-5821-7 (lib. bdg.)

For information on and a full description of any Time-Life Books series, please write:
Reader Information
Time-Life Books
541 North Fairbanks Court
Chicago, Illinois 60611

Time-Life Books Inc. offers a wide range of fine recordings, including a *Big Bands* series. For subscription information, call 1-800-621-7026, or write TIME-LIFE MUSIC, Time & Life Building, Chicago, Illinois 60611.

HEALTHY HOME COOKING

SERIES DIRECTOR: Dale M. Brown
Deputy Editor: Barbara Fleming
Series Administrator: Elise Ritter Gibson
Designer: Herbert H. Quarmby
Picture Editor: Sally Collins
Photographer: Renée Comet
Text Editor: Allan Fallow
Editorial Assistant: Rebecca C. Christoffersen

Editorial Staff for *Fresh Ways with Soups & Stews:*
Book Manager: Jean Getlein
Assistant Picture Editor: Scarlet Cheng
Researcher/Writer: Barbara Sause
Writer: Margery A. duMond
Copy Coordinators: Elizabeth Graham, Norma Karlin
Picture Coordinator: Linda Yates
Photographer's Assistant: Rina M. Ganassa

Special Contributors: Mary Jane Blandford (food purchasing), Carol Gvozdich (nutrient analysis), Nancy Lendved (props), Tajvana Queen (kitchen assistant), Ann Ready (text), CiCi Williamson (microwave section)

THE COOKS

ADAM DE VITO began his cooking apprenticeship at L'Auberge Chez François near Washington, D.C., when he was only 14. He has worked at Washington's Le Pavillon restaurant, taught with cookbook author Madeleine Kamman, and conducted classes at L'Académie de Cuisine in Maryland.

HENRY GROSSI, who started his cooking career with a New York caterer, earned a Grand Diplôme at the École de Cuisine La Varenne in Paris. He then served as the school's assistant director and as its North American business and publications coordinator.

JOHN T. SHAFFER is a graduate of The Culinary Institute of America at Hyde Park, New York. He has had broad experience as a chef, including five years at The Four Seasons Hotel in Washington, D.C., where he was *chef saucier* at Aux Beaux Champs restaurant.

THE CONSULTANT

CAROL CUTLER lives in Washington, D.C., and is the prizewinning author of many cookbooks, including *The Six-Minute Soufflé and Other Culinary Delights* and *Pâté: The New Main Course for the 80's*. During the 12 years she lived in France, she studied at the Cordon Bleu and the École des Trois Gourmandes, as well as with private chefs. She is a member of the Cercle des Gourmettes and a charter member and past president of Les Dames d'Escoffier.

THE NUTRITION CONSULTANT

JANET TENNEY has been involved in nutrition and consumer affairs since she received her master's degree in human nutrition from Columbia University. She is the manager for developing and implementing nutritional programs for a major chain of supermarkets in the Washington, D.C., area.

Nutritional analyses for *Fresh Ways with Soups & Stews* were derived from Practorcare's Nutriplanner System and other current data.

Other Publications:

UNDERSTANDING COMPUTERS
YOUR HOME
THE ENCHANTED WORLD
THE KODAK LIBRARY OF CREATIVE PHOTOGRAPHY
GREAT MEALS IN MINUTES
THE CIVIL WAR
PLANET EARTH
COLLECTOR'S LIBRARY OF THE CIVIL WAR
THE EPIC OF FLIGHT
THE GOOD COOK
WORLD WAR II
HOME REPAIR AND IMPROVEMENT
THE OLD WEST

This volume is one of a series of illustrated cookbooks that emphasize the preparation of healthful dishes for today's weight-conscious, nutrition-minded eaters.

Fresh Ways
with Soups & Stews

BY

THE EDITORS OF TIME-LIFE BOOKS

TIME-LIFE BOOKS / ALEXANDRIA, VIRGINIA

Contents

Sustenance for Body and Soul 7

The Key to Better Eating 8
Finales with a Flourish 9
Homemade Stocks: Foundations of Flavor 10
Vegetable Stock 10
Chicken Stock 10
Veal Stock 10
Brown Stock 11
Fish Stock 11

Gazpacho Blanco

Quick Stocks from Supplies at Hand 11

1 A Soup for All Settings 13

Caramelized Shallot Soup 14
Black Bean, Bourbon and Ham Soup 15
Sweet Potato and Vegetable Soup 16
Bread Soup 17
Mushroom Soup with Sherry 18
Dilly Avocado Soup 19
Curried Buttermilk and Zucchini Soup 20
Leek, Celery and Gruyère Soup 20
Puréeing: Why and How 20
Tomato Purée with Yogurt-Ricotta Stars 22
Scallion Soup 23
Tarragon-Zucchini Soup 24
Black-Eyed Pea and Collard Green Soup 25

Green Pea Soup with Smoked Salmon 26
Beet and Parsnip Soup 27
Vegetable-Broth Minestrone 28
Gazpacho Blanco 29
Onion and Red Potato Soup with Walnut Toasts 30
Cold Curried Vegetable Soup 31
Cold Parsley Soup with Icy Tomato Granita 33
Corn and Cilantro Soup 33
Cabbage and Caraway Soup 34
Hot and Sour Soup 35
Puréed Cauliflower Soup 36
Cauliflower Soup Provençale 37
Curried Yellow Split Pea Soup with Lamb and Mint 39
Caraway-Flavored Celeriac Soup 39
Escarole Soup with Turnips and Apple 40
Peppery Peanut Soup 41
White Bean Soup Cooked with a Bulb of Garlic 42
Chestnut Soup 43
Gazpacho with Roasted Peppers 44
Roquefort Onion Soup 45
Cream of Carrot Soup with Fresh Ginger 46
Chilled Curried Cucumber Soup 46
Turnip Soup 48
Consommé 49

Turkey Soup with Lemon-Celery Dumplings

A Simple Way to Clarify Stock 49
Edible Adornments for Consommé 50
Beef and Capellini Soup with Scallions and Red Pepper 52
Chicken Soup with Carrots, Potatoes and Spinach 53
Duck Soup with Endive and Caramelized Pears 54
Degreasing Soups and Stews 55
Skinning a Duck 55

Veal and Noodle Soup with Sage 56
Sake-Simmered Velvet Chicken Soup 56
Lamb and Wild-Rice Soup 58
Chicken, Eggplant and Tomato Soup 59
Chicken Soup with Chilies, Cabbage and Rice 60
Beef Soup with Brussels Sprouts and Sweet Potato 61
Pork Soup with Nappa Cabbage 61
Turkey-Lentil Soup 62
Lamb Broth with Winter Vegetables 63
Vegetable Soup with Grilled Chicken 64
Turkey Goulash Soup 65
Turkey Soup with Lemon-Celery Dumplings 66
Beef and Wild Mushroom Soup 67
Couscous Soup with Harissa 68
Crab, Fennel and Tomato Soup 69
Key West Conch Chowder 70
Striped Bass and Sweet Pepper Soup 71
Oyster Soup with Watercress and Carrot 72
Clam and Rice Soup 72
Spinach and Fish Soup 74
Shanghai Scallop Soup with 20 Garlic Cloves 75
Chilled Tomato-and-Shrimp Soup 76
Mussel and Artichoke Chowder 77

Green Pea Soup with Smoked Salmon

Fish Soup with Red-Pepper Sauce 78
Oyster Soup with Leeks 79
Hot and Sweet Soup with
Seafood Dumplings........................80
A Fine Kettle of Fish.........................81
Thai Shrimp Soup with
Lemon Grass..................................82
Corn, Scallop and Fettuccine Soup....84
Vietnamese Crab-and-
Asparagus Soup 85
Gingery Pear Soup 86
Golden Gazpacho 86
Peach Soup Flambé 87

Java Lamb Curry with Tamarind 99
Chicken Stew with Zucchini
and Tomatoes 100
Tangerine Beef Stew 101
Veal Stew with Red, Green and
Yellow Peppers 102

Rabbit Stew with Prunes 103
Rabbit Stew with Sherry..................105
Duck Stew with Watercress 106
Lamb-Spinach Stew with Orzo 107
Veal Stew with Pearl Onions and
Grainy Mustard 108

Squid and Red-Bean Stew 123
Caribbean Red-Snapper Stew 123
Shrimp Creole 124
Flounder Curry 125
Trout Stew with Zucchini, Capers
and Watercress 126
Lobster Navarin 127
Turning Vegetables to
Elegant Effect...............................128
Seafood Chili with Peppers and
Tomatillos 128

2 Stew's Ever-Constant Magic 89

Sherried Vegetable Potpourri............90
Vegetable Stew with Okra 91
Sweet Potato Stew...........................92
Vegetable Stew, East Indian Style 92
Chunky Beef Chili 94
Lentil-Sausage Stew 95
Chilies — A Cautionary Note............95
Turkey Stew with Mediterranean
Vegetables.....................................96
Chicken Gumbo..............................97

Mediterranean Fish Chowder

3 Soups and Stews in the Microwave 131

Light Vegetable Stew with
Snow Peas and Mustard 131
Gingery Acorn Squash Soup 132
Sweet-and-Sour Fish Stew 133
Pork and Bean-Sprout Soup............135
Seafood Stew in Garlic-
Tomato Sauce 135
Chicken Stew with Mashed
Potatoes 136
Broccoli Soup with Cumin and
Bay Scallops 137
Cold Apple-and-Tarragon Soup 138

Mexican Chicken Stew with
Ancho Chilies 108
Pork and Apple Stew 110
Oxtails Braised with Carrots 111
A Cut above the Rest.....................112
Sauerbraten Stew with
Candied Ginger.............................113
Beef Stew with Stout 114
Chicken Stew in Whole Green and
Red Peppers 114
Beef Stew with Apricots and
Couscous 116
Seafood Stew with Water
Chestnuts 117
Southwest Gumbo 118
Cod Stewed with Onions,
Potatoes, Corn and Tomatoes........119
Mediterranean Fish Chowder 120
Smoked and Fresh Salmon in
Red Wine Stew.............................121

Sweet-and-Sour Fish Stew

Chicken Ratatouille 138

Glossary 140
Index 141
Picture Credits and
Acknowledgments.......................144

Duck Stew with Watercress

Sustenance for Body and Soul

Soups and stews are time-honored comfort foods, with rounded, blended flavors and soothing, sustaining warmth. Prepared more often than not in a single pot, they can incorporate all kinds of ingredients in combinations that are as nutritious as they are delicious. As the contents cook, tendrils of steam and aroma curl up, permeating the surroundings and inducing a sense of well-being. What dreary winter afternoon is not brightened by the companionable murmur of a simmering soup on the stove? What kitchen is not cheered by the rich scent of a bubbling beef stew?

Soups and stews have much in common, yet there is more to set them apart than the spoon or fork used to eat them. A soup can be thin or thick; it can range from a clear, light broth to a hearty chowder. A stew, on the other hand, possesses more body, and its components are likely to be chunkier. A soup can serve as a first course, a main course or — when made with fruit — even a dessert. It can also be a between-meal snack. A stew, however, often constitutes a meal in itself.

Stock, the basis of it all

What soups and stews share is their basic method of preparation. Both, of course, require a liquid — be it stock, wine or water — in which everything cooks. Indeed, a good, flavorful stock is at the core of most soup and stew making. Recipes for five stocks — chicken, fish, vegetable, veal and brown — follow this introduction. Not least of their many benefits is the opportunity they present for economy; some of the ingredients — such as chicken bones and trimmings, which can be accumulated in the freezer — yield goodness that might otherwise have been squandered.

Stocks may be stored in the refrigerator for several days, or kept in the freezer for up to four months. (The exception is fish stock, which should be stored no longer than two months.) Once frozen, a stock may be removed from its container and tightly sealed in a plastic freezer bag, then labeled, dated, and returned to the freezer. Alternatively, it may be poured into a plastic bag fitted inside a container and removed when frozen.

Soups and stews are eminently practical. Almost anything edible can find its way into the pot, though the freshest ingredients produce the tastiest dishes. And because they cook in liquid that is consumed rather than discarded, soups and stews preserve most of the nutrients that escape from the ingredients themselves during cooking. Only a heat-sensitive vitamin like C is at risk here, and foods rich in it, such as broccoli, green peppers and Brussels sprouts, ideally should be added toward the end.

Besides offering sound nourishment, the 117 soups and stews in this book boast reduced levels of sodium, fat and cholesterol. The stocks specified in the recipes are all unsalted, freeing the cook to use a small amount of salt later, when it can most effectively contribute its flavor. Many of the dishes are degreased; a box on page 55 describes several methods for doing so. Where egg yolks, cream or flour may traditionally have been employed as thickening agents, vegetable purées are often incorporated instead, contributing the requisite smoothness and body.

Soups in themselves can play a role in weight control. They take some time to eat, especially when they are served piping hot, and they can be pleasantly filling. Moreover, the lighter, thinner ones possess fewer calories per mouthful than most other dishes, yet they offer just as much satisfaction. All this adds up to an unexpected bonus. Scientists tell us that hunger is at least partially in our heads: The brain, they say, receives a signal when the body needs nourishment; it receives another signal as soon as that need has been met. As anyone with an appetite knows, it is all too easy to wolf down food. But when we start a meal with a hot soup, taking it in slowly as we must — spoonful by spoonful — our brain receives the message that our appetite has been curbed before we can overindulge.

In addition to their healthful advantages, soups and stews qualify as convenience dishes — and not just because they normally cook in one pot. Often they demand little effort beyond the initial preparation of the ingredients, and little watching. And because most cook slowly — particularly stews — tough cuts of meat respond by turning tender. Tomatoes or wine introduce acids that further help break down tissue. The liquid must never be allowed to boil rapidly, though, for high heat can dry out meat and make it stringy. Be particularly careful to cook such white meats as chicken and veal at a simmer; seafood, if it is not to toughen, should be cooked for as little time as possible.

The preferred vessel for cooking soups and stews is a heavy-bottomed pot or casserole, with even heat distribution and enough capacity to hold the soup or stew without spillage. For six portions, a 4-quart pot will do. Where appropriate, use the lid to regulate the temperature of the mixture as it cooks. And bear in mind that certain metals, among them iron and aluminum, react with the acids in foods, or in wine and vinegar, causing discoloration and bitterness. A nonreactive pot, made of stainless steel or coated with such a substance as enamel, prevents this.

For making stock, a stockpot is ideal. The tall sides encourage the stock to circulate, allowing the heated liquid to rise to the top and displace the cooler liquid there. The pot's tubular shape also makes for a small surface area, ensuring controlled evaporation during the long simmering that is essential to most good stocks.

Fortunately, the preparation of stocks, soups and stews requires no other specialized equipment. Puréeing can be accomplished with a sieve and the back of a wooden spoon, with an old-fashioned food mill, or with a blender or food processor. Each of the electric appliances has its special applications; the blender,

The Key to Better Eating

Healthy Home Cooking addresses the concerns of today's weight-conscious, health-minded cooks with recipes that take into account guidelines set by nutritionists. The secret to eating well, of course, has to do with maintaining a balance of foods in the diet. The recipes thus should be used thoughtfully, in the context of a day's eating, and not just with regard to the meal being prepared. To make the choice easier, this book presents an analysis of nutrients in a single serving of each soup or stew recipe, as at right. Approximate counts for calories, protein, cholesterol, total fat, saturated fat and sodium are given.

Interpreting the chart

The chart below presents the National Research Council's Recommended Dietary Allowances of both calories and protein for healthy men, women and children of average size, along with the council's recommendations for the "safe and adequate" maximum intake of sodium. Although the council has not established similar recommendations for either cholesterol or fat, the chart does include what the National Institutes of Health and the American Heart Association consider the maximum allowable amounts of these in one day's eating by healthy members of the general population.

The volumes in the Healthy Home Cooking series do not purport to be diet books, nor do they focus on health foods. Rather, the books express a commonsense approach to cooking that uses salt, sugar, cream, butter and oil in moderation while employing other ingredients that also contribute flavor and satisfaction. Herbs, spices and aromatic vegetables, as well as fruits, peels, juices, wines and vinegars are all used toward this end. The portions themselves are modest in size.

The recipes make few unusual demands. Naturally they call for fresh ingredients, offering substitutes when these are unavailable. (Only the original ingredient is calculat-

Calories **180**
Protein **21g.**
Cholesterol **65mg.**
Total fat **8g.**
Saturated fat **4g.**
Sodium **230mg.**

ed in the nutrient analysis, however.) Most of the ingredients can be found in any well-stocked supermarket; the occasional exceptions can usually be bought in specialty shops or ethnic stores.

A glossary on pages 140 and 141 describes and defines any unusual ingredients. In instances where particular techniques may be unfamiliar to a cook, photographs and instructions explain them.

In Healthy Home Cooking's test kitchens, heavy-bottomed pots and pans are used to guard against burning the food whenever a small amount of oil is used and where there is the possible danger of the food adhering to the hot surface, but nonstick pans can be utilized as well.

Both safflower oil and pure olive oil are favored by the cooks for sautéing. Safflower oil was chosen because it is the most highly polyunsaturated vegetable fat available in supermarkets, and polyunsaturated fats reduce blood cholesterol. Where flavor is important, virgin olive oil is used because it has a fine fruity taste that is lacking in the pure grade. Olive oil is high in monounsaturated fats, which do not increase blood cholesterol and, according to recent research, may even help to lower it.

About cooking times

To help the cook plan ahead, Healthy Home Cooking takes time into account in all its recipes. While recognizing that everyone cooks at a different speed, and that stoves and ovens may differ somewhat in their temperatures, the series provides approximate "working" and "total" times for every dish. Working time stands for the minutes actively spent on preparation; total time includes unattended cooking time, as well as time devoted to marinating, steeping or soaking ingredients. Since the recipes emphasize fresh foods, they may take a bit longer to prepare than "quick and easy" dishes that call for canned or packaged products, but the payoff in flavor, and often in nutrition, should compensate for the little extra time involved.

Recommended Dietary Guidelines

		Average Daily Intake		Maximum Daily Intake			
		CALORIES	PROTEIN grams	CHOLESTEROL milligrams	TOTAL FAT grams	SATURATED FAT grams	SODIUM milligrams
Children	7-10	2400	22	240	80	27	1800
Females	11-14	2200	37	220	73	24	2700
	15-18	2100	44	210	70	23	2700
	19-22	2100	44	300	70	23	3300
	23-50	2000	44	300	67	22	3300
	51-75	1800	44	300	60	20	3300
Males	11-14	2700	36	270	90	30	2700
	15-18	2800	56	280	93	31	2700
	19-22	2900	56	300	97	32	3300
	23-50	2700	56	300	90	30	3300
	51-75	2400	56	300	80	27	3300

for example, yields a more homogenized purée *(box, page 20)*. The recipes in this book offer the cook choices, but the device considered best for the job is always listed first.

Many soups and stews can be prepared in advance. To inhibit bacterial growth, they should be refrigerated, partially covered, within half an hour. One of stew's endearing qualities is that it often tastes better the next day, when flavors have had a chance to mingle and blend still more. With a microwave oven, this trait becomes doubly attractive: A stew made ahead of time and stored overnight in the refrigerator will have deliciously matured, needing only brief reheating in the microwave.

Soups and stews can be stored in the freezer for as long as three months. But be careful: Many seafood and vegetable soups do not freeze well — potatoes, for instance, turn mushy. And remember that soups and stews will lose some of their flavor and texture during the freezing process, and a little of their nutritive value when warmed. Thaw soups and stews gradually in the refrigerator, then gently reheat them.

How this book is organized

The recipes appearing in the first section of the book are all soups, and they are grouped according to their principal ingredient — vegetables, seafood, meat (including poultry) and fruit. Most are to be served hot, but many can be enjoyed cold. The second section is devoted to stews, likewise grouped according to main ingredient. The third section presents microwave recipes for both soups and stews.

The nutrient analysis accompanying each recipe is based on a single serving of the dish. For a soup that is to be consumed as a first course, the portion size can range from six to 10 ounces — about a cupful. As with all good menu planning, the cook should try to gauge how rich or lean the rest of the meal will be before selecting a first-course soup. For a soup that is intended as a main course, the serving size is naturally larger — 10 to 12 ounces, or about a cup and a half.

Finishing touches

The cook's creative possibilities do not evaporate with the curling steam of a finished soup or stew. A main-course soup may require an accompaniment or a garnish such as croutons *(box, right)* to round out its nutritional value or to enhance its visual appeal. Often, such low-fat accompaniments as soda crackers, Scandinavian crisp breads, melba toast, a chunk of crusty bread, or a slice of rye or pumpernickel will be enough to furnish the required starch. Similarly, nutritional balance may be achieved by eating a meat stew with bread, noodles or dumplings, along with a salad of fresh vegetables. A vegetable stew may be served with

a small helping of meat or cheese, a salad of beans or lentils, or a milk dessert such as custard.

Where you can, match the type of bowl to the character of the soup, using delicate porcelain or glass for a clear consommé, say, and rustic pottery for stews. To hold the food at the appropriate temperature, warm the bowls for hot concoctions and chill them for cold ones. A tureen with a lid — the tureen gently heated with hot water before the soup or stew goes in — lends the dish presence at the table, acknowledging that food as good and sustaining as this deserves attention.

Finales with a Flourish

Homemade croutons add the finishing touch to soup — and, when cut into fanciful shapes, they offer unlimited improvisation on the standard cube of bread. Because the croutons are cooked without oil — the bread pieces are simply toasted in an oven or beneath a broiler — they make healthful additions to whatever dish they adorn: smooth, creamy soups, chilled gazpacho, seafood soups or stews, even a hearty bean soup.

Use white bread or dark, but select a homemade-style loaf for its fine texture. To make traditional croutons, use a serrated knife to cut a slice of bread into strips ½ to 1 inch wide, then cut the strips crosswise into squares. For triangular croutons, further cut each square in half on the diagonal. To produce the unusual profiles pictured above, use an aspic cutter or a jelly cutter. Arrange the pieces on a baking sheet and set them in a preheated 350° F. oven until they turn golden brown *(above, lower tray)* — about 20 minutes.

To give new life to stale loaves of French bread, cut them into croûtes — small rounds of toast *(above, upper tray)*. For variation, slice each round in half and scoop out the centers, forming crescents, or simply cut the crust alone into rectangles or squares. Toast the croûtes under the broiler, then float them in individual servings of soup. To add flavor along with the crunch, rub a peeled clove of garlic over each croûte.

Homemade Stocks: Foundations of Flavor

A soup or stew is only as good as the stock on which it is built — and happily, making good stock is a simple procedure. The ingredients are simmered in a pot; when strained and degreased *(box, page 55)*, the cooking liquid becomes a savory essence to serve on its own, store for later use, or elaborate into another dish. Recipes for five basic stocks appear at right.

The elixir that is stock comes from humble beginnings indeed — inexpensive cuts of meat, fish bones, or chicken wings and backs. Attention to details will reward you with a rich and beautifully limpid stock: Any large fat deposits should be trimmed away beforehand; large bones, if they are to cede the treasured gelatin that gives body to a stock, should be cracked first. During cooking, remove the scum that collects occasionally atop the liquid. Scum consists of protein particles released by meat and bones; these float to the surface, where they gather in a foam. As nutritious as it is, the foam must be removed lest it cloud the stock. Skim off the scum as it forms at the start of cooking; skim thereafter only as the recipe directs. After its initial rapid cooking, a stock must not be allowed to return to a full boil; the turbulence would muddy the liquid. As a final cleansing, the stock should be strained through a fine sieve or a colander lined with cheesecloth.

To prepare stock for storage, divide it among containers surrounded with ice water. Wait until the stock has cooled to cover the vessels; otherwise, it may sour. Refrigerated in covered containers, any of these stocks will keep for up to three days. Because the fat atop the stock will form a temporary seal, helping to keep it fresh, you need not degrease the stock until shortly before you are ready to use it. To prolong the life of a refrigerated stock, first remove and discard the congealed fat, then boil the stock for five minutes; either freeze the stock or boil it again every two or three days. As always, cool it quickly — and uncovered — before storing it once more.

Fish stock and vegetable stock may be frozen for two months; the other three may be frozen for as long as four months. Stock destined for the freezer must first be degreased; frozen fat can turn rancid.

The recipes that follow yield differing amounts of stock. Brown stock and veal stock, for example, are made from large bones, which require more water for cooking. But like any stock, these two freeze well, meaning an abundance is never too much.

Vegetable Stock

Makes about 2 quarts
Working time: about 25 minutes
Total time: about 1 hour and 30 minutes

4 celery stalks with leaves, cut into 1-inch pieces
4 carrots, scrubbed and cut into 1-inch pieces
4 large onions (about 2 lb.), coarsely chopped
3 large broccoli stems (optional), coarsely chopped
1 medium turnip, peeled and cut into ½-inch cubes
6 garlic cloves, crushed
½ cup coarsely chopped parsley leaves and stems
10 black peppercorns
4 fresh thyme sprigs, or 1 tsp. dried thyme leaves
2 bay leaves, crumbled

Put the celery, carrots, onions, broccoli if you are using it, turnip, garlic, parsley and peppercorns into a heavy stockpot. Pour in enough cold water to cover the contents by about 2 inches. Bring the liquid to a boil over medium heat, skimming off any scum that rises to the surface. When the liquid reaches a boil, stir in the thyme and the bay leaves. Reduce the heat and let the stock simmer undisturbed for one hour.

Strain the stock into a large bowl, pressing down lightly on the vegetables to extract all their liquid. Discard the vegetables.

Chicken Stock

Makes about 2 quarts
Working time: about 20 minutes
Total time: about 3 hours

4 to 5 lb. uncooked chicken trimmings and bones (preferably wings, necks and backs), the bones cracked with a heavy knife
2 carrots, cut into ½-inch-thick rounds
2 celery stalks, cut into 1-inch pieces
2 large onions (about 1 lb.), cut in half, one half stuck with 2 cloves
2 fresh thyme sprigs, or ½ tsp. dried thyme leaves
1 or 2 bay leaves
10 to 15 parsley stems
5 black peppercorns

Put the chicken trimmings and bones into a heavy stockpot; pour in enough water to cover them by about 2 inches. Bring the liquid to a boil over medium heat, skimming off the scum that rises to the surface. Reduce the heat and simmer the liquid for 10 minutes, skimming and adding a little cold water to help precipitate the scum.

Add the vegetables, herbs and peppercorns, and submerge them in the liquid. If necessary, pour in enough additional water to cover the contents of the pot. Simmer the stock for two to three hours, skimming as necessary to remove the scum.

Strain the stock, discard the solids, and degrease the stock *(box, page 55)*.

EDITOR'S NOTE: *The chicken gizzard and heart may be added to the stock. Wings and necks — rich in natural gelatin — produce a particularly gelatinous stock, ideal for sauces and jellied dishes.*
Turkey, duck or goose stock may be prepared using the same basic recipe.

Veal Stock

Makes about 3 quarts
Working time: about 30 minutes
Total time: about 4½ hours

3 lb. veal breast or shank meat, cut into 3-inch pieces
3 lb. veal bones (preferably knuckles), cracked
2 onions, quartered

2 celery stalks, sliced
1 carrot, sliced
8 black peppercorns
3 unpeeled garlic cloves (optional), crushed
1 tsp. fresh thyme, or ¼ tsp. dried thyme leaves
1 bay leaf

Fill a large pot halfway with water. Bring the water to a boil, add the veal meat and bones, and blanch them for two minutes to clean them. Drain the meat and bones in a colander, discarding the liquid. Rinse the meat and bones under cold running water and return them to the pot.

Add the onions, celery, carrot, peppercorns, and garlic if you are using it. Pour in enough water to cover the contents of the pot by about 3 inches, and bring the water to a boil over medium heat. Reduce the heat to maintain a simmer, and skim any impurities from the surface. Add the thyme and bay leaf, and simmer the stock very gently for four hours, skimming occasionally.

Strain the stock into a large bowl; allow the solids to drain thoroughly into the bowl before discarding them. Degrease the stock (box, page 55).

EDITOR'S NOTE: Any combination of veal meat and bones may be used to make this stock; ideally, the meat and bones together should weigh about six pounds. Ask your butcher to crack the bones.

Brown Stock

Makes about 3 quarts
Working time: about 40 minutes
Total time: about 5½ hours

3 lb. veal breast (or veal-shank or beef-shank meat), cut into 3-inch pieces
3 lb. uncooked veal or beef bones, cracked
2 onions, quartered
2 celery stalks, chopped
2 carrots, sliced
3 unpeeled garlic cloves, crushed
8 black peppercorns
3 cloves
2 tsp. fresh thyme, or ½ tsp. dried thyme leaves
1 bay leaf

Preheat the oven to 425° F. Place the meat, bones, onions, celery and carrots in a large roasting pan and roast them in the oven until they are well browned — about one hour.

Transfer the contents of the roasting pan to a large pot. Pour 2 cups of water into the roasting pan; with a spatula, scrape up the browned bits from the bottom of the pan. Pour the liquid into the pot.

Add the garlic, peppercorns and cloves. Pour in enough water to cover the contents of the pot by about 3 inches. Bring the liquid to a boil, then reduce the heat to maintain a simmer and skim any impurities from the surface. Add the thyme and bay leaf, then simmer the stock very gently for four hours, skimming occasionally during the process.

Strain the stock; allow the solids to drain thoroughly into the stock before discarding them. Degrease the stock (box, page 55).

EDITOR'S NOTE: Thoroughly browning the meat,

Quick Stocks from Supplies at Hand

Canned stocks are no substitute for home-made, but they can be used in a pinch. A handful of readily available ingredients will invigorate them. Similar treatment will transform bottled clam juice into a creditable fish stock.

To enliven canned beef stock (called broth or bouillon), combine several table-spoons each of minced onion and carrot and a tablespoon or two of minced celery with 2 cans of stock. Next pour in ½ cup of red or dry white wine and 2½ cups of water, then add two sprigs of parsley, a small bay leaf and a pinch of dried thyme. Simmer the mixture for 20 to 30 minutes, then strain and degrease it (box, page 55).

To add spark to two cans of low-sodium chicken broth, use vegetables and herbs in the same proportion as for beef stock, but do not add water; instead use ¼ cup of white wine. If you wish, toss in a few celery leaves. Simmer the stock for 20 to 30 minutes, then strain it. In the case of beef stock, a good low-sodium stock is unavailable, so reduce or omit the salt in the recipe.

To every 2 cups of clam juice, add 1 cup of water, ½ cup of dry white wine, a sliced onion and four black peppercorns. (Be sure to reduce or omit the salt in the dish.) Simmer the stock for 10 minutes, then strain it.

bones and vegetables should produce a stock with a rich mahogany color. If your stock does not seem dark enough, cook 1 tablespoon of tomato paste in a small pan over medium heat, stirring constantly, until it darkens — about three minutes. Add this to the stock about one hour before the end of the cooking time.

Any combination of meat and bones may be used to make the stock; ideally, the meat and bones together should weigh about six pounds. Ask your butcher to crack the bones.

Fish Stock

Makes about 2 quarts
Working time: about 15 minutes
Total time: about 40 minutes

2 lb. lean-fish bones, fins and tails discarded, the bones rinsed thoroughly and cut into large pieces
2 onions, thinly sliced
2 celery stalks, chopped
1 carrot, thinly sliced
2 cups dry white wine
2 tbsp. fresh lemon juice
1 leek (optional), trimmed, split, washed thoroughly to remove all grit, and sliced
3 garlic cloves (optional), crushed
10 parsley stems
4 fresh thyme sprigs, or 1 tsp. dried thyme leaves
1 bay leaf, crumbled
5 black peppercorns

Put the fish bones, onions, celery, carrot, wine, lemon juice, 2 quarts of cold water, and the leek and garlic if you are using them, in a large, nonreactive stockpot. Bring the liquid to a boil over medium heat, then reduce the heat to maintain a strong simmer. Skim off all the scum that rises to the surface.

Add the parsley, thyme, bay leaf and peppercorns, and gently simmer the stock for 20 minutes more.

Strain the stock; allow the solids to drain thoroughly before discarding them. If necessary, degrease the stock (box, page 55).

EDITOR'S NOTE: Because the bones from oilier fish produce a strong flavor, be sure to use only the bones from lean fish. Sole, flounder, turbot and other flatfish are best. Do not include the fish skin; it could discolor the stock.

1 *Thinly sliced sautéed mushrooms float lightly in a sherry-enriched soup that contains just 140 calories per serving (recipe, page 18).*

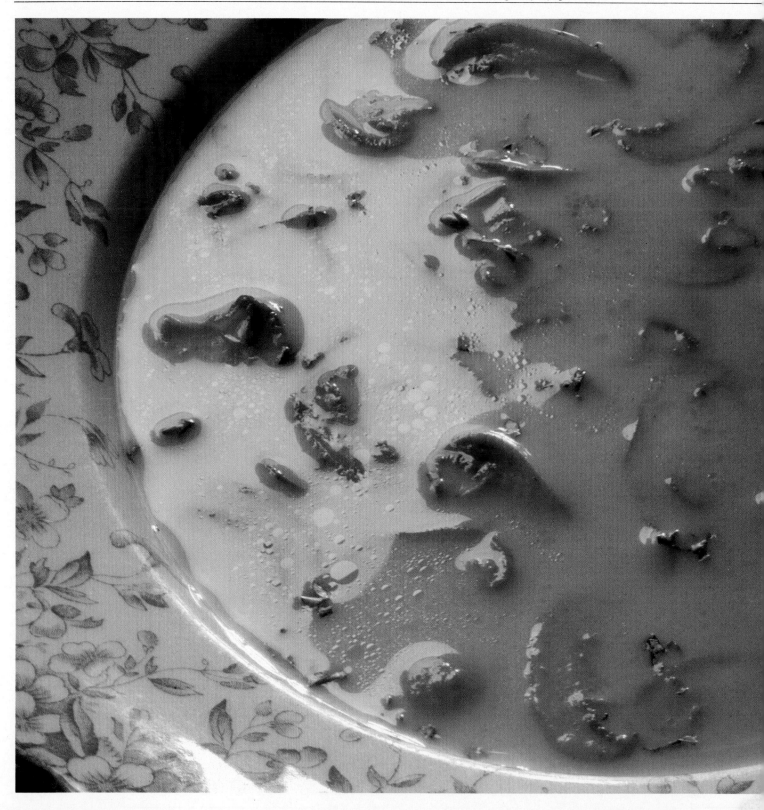

A Soup for All Settings

In the *grande cuisine* propounded at the turn of the century, one axiom was that soup should not be omitted from the evening meal. We are fortunate to live in an era of less exacting rules, when soup may appear at almost any time of day and in almost any position on the menu — from snack to entree, from appetizer to dessert. Indeed, soups may even constitute an entire meal. Restaurateur George Lang once had the audacity to serve his dinner guests a four-course meal of soups; he was somewhat chagrined to learn afterward that a similar menu had been devised four centuries earlier — but in five courses.

This section offers soups of all types for all occasions. The majority are built upon one of the five stock recipes that appear on pages 10 and 11. But there are stockless soups too. Most of the recipes are simple to prepare, and some require only a minimum investment of time. The corn-and-cilantro soup on page 33, for instance, is ready in 20 minutes. Similarly, Vietnamese Crab-and-Asparagus Soup *(page 85)* takes but half an hour. And the cold avocado soup with fresh dill on page 19 can be prepared in 15 minutes; after an hour's chilling, it is ready to eat.

Many of the recipes were developed as updated versions of familiar concoctions. The beet soup on page 27, for example, is a fresh variation on borscht; to provide greater diversity of flavor and to subtract much of the fat and sodium found in the customary rendition, it includes lemon juice, parsnips and an apple. Caramelized Shallot Soup *(page 14)* presents a flavorful departure from the classic French onion soup; a splash of balsamic vinegar adds depth and greatly diminishes the amount of salt required. The peanut soup on page 41, meanwhile, contains only one fourth the fat of its Southern prototype; as a result it is a lighter version that satisfies without cloying. And the bread soup on page 17, while paying homage to the past and to one of the most venerable soups of all, cuts down on the oil and egg yolks that some consider essential to the dish; instead, flavor is built up by the inclusion of kale and chicken stock.

Caramelized Shallot Soup

Serves 4 as a first course
Working time: about 45 minutes
Total time: about 1 hour

Calories **190**
Protein **4g.**
Cholesterol **9mg.**
Total fat **7g.**
Saturated fat **2g.**
Sodium **245mg.**

1 tbsp. unsalted butter
1 tbsp. safflower oil
1 lb. shallots, peeled and thinly sliced
¼ tsp. salt
freshly ground black pepper
½ cup dry vermouth or dry white wine
¼ cup balsamic vinegar, or 3 tbsp. red wine vinegar mixed with 1 tsp. honey
2 garlic cloves, finely chopped
4 cups unsalted veal stock, reduced to 2½ cups
1 tbsp. chopped fresh mint

Heat the butter and oil together in a large, heavy-bottomed pot over medium heat. Add the shallots, salt and some pepper. Cook the shallots, scraping the bottom of the pot often to prevent the shallots from burning, until they are caramelized — about 30 minutes.

Add the vermouth or white wine, the balsamic vinegar or wine vinegar and honey, and the garlic; cook for two minutes, scraping up the caramelized bits from the bottom of the pan. Pour in the stock and bring the liquid to a simmer. Reduce the heat and simmer the soup for 15 minutes. Stir in the mint before serving.

Black Bean, Bourbon and Ham Soup

Serves 6
Working time: about 1 hour and 30 minutes
Total time: about 3 hours (includes soaking)

Calories **365**	1 lb. black beans, picked over
Protein **24g.**	1 lb. smoked ham hocks
Cholesterol **14mg.**	3 cups chopped onion
Total fat **5g.**	5 garlic cloves, chopped
Saturated fat **1g.**	1½ tsp. dried thyme leaves
Sodium **215mg.**	½ tsp. ground cumin
	freshly ground black pepper
	3 tbsp. sour cream
	⅓ cup plain low-fat yogurt
	1 scallion, trimmed and finely chopped
	¼ cup bourbon or sour-mash whiskey

Rinse the beans under cold running water, then put them into a large pot and pour in enough cold water to cover them by about 3 inches. Discard any beans that float to the surface. Cover the pot, leaving the lid ajar, and slowly bring the liquid to a boil over medium-low heat. Boil the beans for two minutes, then turn off the heat and soak the beans, covered, for at least one hour. (Alternatively, soak the beans in cold water overnight.)

Place the ham hocks in a large, heavy-bottomed pot. Pour in 14 cups of water and bring it to a boil. Cook the ham hocks over high heat for 20 minutes, skimming off any impurities that collect on the surface.

Drain the beans and add them to the pot with the ham hocks. Return the mixture to a boil and cook it for 15 minutes more, stirring from time to time and skimming any foam from the surface.

Reduce the heat to medium. Add the onion, garlic, thyme, cumin and some pepper. Simmer the soup, stirring occasionally and skimming any foam from the surface, until the beans are tender — one and a half to two hours.

While the beans are cooking, whisk together the sour cream, yogurt and scallion; set the mixture aside.

When the beans finish cooking, remove the soup from the heat. With tongs or a slotted spoon, take out the ham hocks and set them aside to cool. When the ham hocks are cool enough to handle, separate the meat from the skin and bones by hand. Cut the meat into small pieces and return it to the soup; discard the skin and bones.

Whisk in the bourbon or sour-mash whiskey and bring the soup to a boil. Remove the pot from the heat and ladle the soup into bowls; garnish each portion with a dollop of the sour-cream-yogurt mixture.

Sweet Potato and Vegetable Soup

Serves 6 as a first course
Working time: about 45 minutes
Total time: about 2 hours

Calories **95**
Protein **4g.**
Cholesterol **0mg.**
Total fat **1g.**
Saturated fat **0g.**
Sodium **105mg.**

2 large sweet potatoes (about 1 lb.), scrubbed
1 small cauliflower (about 1¼ lb.), cored and cut into florets, the core and leaves reserved
3 onions (about 1 lb.), 2 of them thinly sliced, the other cut into small chunks
1 whole garlic bulb, halved horizontally
2 zucchini (about 8 oz.), scrubbed, trimmed and cut into ¾-inch-thick rounds
juice of 1 lemon
freshly ground black pepper
1 tbsp. fresh thyme, or ¾ tsp. dried thyme leaves
1 tsp. whole cloves
½ tsp. ground allspice
¼ tsp. salt

Bake one of the sweet potatoes in a preheated 375° F. oven until it is quite soft — 50 minutes to one hour. (Alternatively, microwave the sweet potato on high for seven minutes. Remove it from the oven, wrap it in aluminum foil, and let it stand for 10 minutes.) When the baked sweet potato is cool enough to handle, peel it and set it aside.

Meanwhile, peel the remaining sweet potato and cut it crosswise into thin slices. Set the slices aside. Cut the cauliflower core into chunks and set the chunks aside with the leaves.

Put the onion slices, cauliflower chunks and leaves (but not the florets), raw sweet-potato slices, garlic, lemon juice and some pepper in a large, nonreactive pot. Pour in 8 cups of water and bring the liquid to a boil. Reduce the heat and simmer the mixture; skim off any impurities that have collected on the surface. Add the thyme and cloves, and continue to simmer the liquid until it is reduced by half — about 40 minutes.

Strain the liquid through a fine sieve into a bowl, pushing down on the vegetables with a wooden spoon to extract all their juices. Return the strained liquid to the pot; discard the solids.

Purée the baked sweet potato in a food processor or blender along with ½ cup of the strained liquid. Whisk the purée into the liquid in the pot. Add the onion chunks, cauliflower florets, allspice, salt and some more pepper. Bring the liquid to a simmer over medium heat and cook it for five minutes. Add the zucchini rounds and cook the soup until the zucchini is tender — seven to 10 minutes more. Serve the soup either hot or cold.

Bread Soup

Serves 4
Working time: about 35 minutes
Total time: about 1 hour

Calories **275**
Protein **10g.**
Cholesterol **6mg.**
Total fat **11g.**
Saturated fat **2g.**
Sodium **605mg.**

1½ cups 1-inch bread cubes, cut from day-old French or Italian bread
2 tbsp. olive oil
1 large leek, trimmed, split, washed thoroughly to remove all grit, and thinly sliced
2 garlic cloves, finely chopped
1 small Belgian endive, trimmed, split lengthwise and sliced crosswise
1 oz. prosciutto (about 2 thin slices), julienned
1 bunch arugula, or 8 oz. fresh kale, washed and stemmed
6 cups unsalted chicken or veal stock
2 boiling potatoes, peeled and diced
5 drops hot red-pepper sauce

½ tsp. salt
½ tsp. crushed black peppercorns

Preheat the oven to 350° F. Arrange the bread cubes in a single layer on a baking sheet and bake them until they are toasted — about 15 minutes.

Heat the oil in a large, heavy-bottomed pot over medium heat. Add the leek and cook it, stirring frequently, until it begins to brown — about 10 minutes. Stir in the garlic, endive and prosciutto, and continue cooking, stirring occasionally, until the endive softens — approximately five minutes. Add the arugula or kale and cover the pot; cook the mixture until the arugula or kale wilts — about three minutes more.

Stir in the stock, potatoes and red-pepper sauce. Reduce the heat, cover the pot and simmer the soup until the potatoes are tender — about 15 minutes.

Stir in the salt, pepper and toasted bread cubes; allow the bread cubes to soak up some of the broth before serving the soup.

Mushroom Soup with Sherry

Serves 4 as a first course
Working (and total) time: about 45 minutes

Calories **140**
Protein **5g.**
Cholesterol **15mg.**
Total fat **8g.**
Saturated fat **3g.**
Sodium **355mg.**

½ tbsp. unsalted butter
½ tbsp. safflower oil
1 onion, thinly sliced
1 lb. mushrooms, wiped clean, trimmed and thinly sliced
4 cups unsalted chicken stock
¼ cup dry sherry
½ tsp. salt
freshly ground black pepper
¼ cup light cream
1 to 2 tbsp. chopped fresh parsley

Melt the butter with the oil in a large, heavy-bottomed or nonstick skillet over medium-high heat. Add the onion and sauté it, stirring often, for four minutes. Add the mushrooms, reduce the heat to medium, and cover the skillet to help the mushrooms release their moisture. Cook the mixture for two minutes, stirring it several times.

Uncover the skillet and increase the heat to medium high. Sauté the mushrooms and onions, stirring from time to time, until all of the moisture has evaporated — about 10 minutes. Continue sautéing, stirring the mixture frequently to prevent sticking, until the mushrooms and onions are golden brown all over — five to 10 minutes more.

Transfer the mushroom mixture to a large saucepan; add the stock, sherry, salt and some pepper. Simmer the soup for 15 minutes. Stir in the cream and the parsley, and allow the soup to heat through before serving.

The soup is better reheated after a mellowing period in the refrigerator. It will keep refrigerated for as long as three days.

Dilly Avocado Soup

Serves 6
Working time: about 15 minutes
Total time: about 1 hour and 15 minutes (includes chilling)

Calories **110**
Protein **5g.**
Cholesterol **5mg.**
Total fat **7g.**
Saturated fat **2g.**
Sodium **165mg.**

1 avocado, halved, peeled and cut into chunks (about 1 cup firmly packed), the pit reserved
2 cups plain low-fat yogurt
1½ cups unsalted chicken stock
2 scallions, trimmed and cut into ¼-inch lengths (about ¼ cup)
1 tbsp. finely cut fresh dill, or ½ tbsp. dried dillweed
¼ tsp. dry mustard
¼ tsp. salt
dill sprigs for garnish (optional)

Put the avocado chunks, yogurt, stock, scallions, cut dill or dillweed, mustard and salt in a blender or food processor and purée the mixture until it is completely smooth. Transfer the soup to a nonreactive container (include the avocado pit, if you like) and tightly cover the container. Chill the soup in the refrigerator for at least one hour. If you wish, garnish each serving with a small sprig of dill.

EDITOR'S NOTE: *Because avocado darkens when exposed to air, cut it just before you purée the soup. The yogurt will help keep the soup from discoloring as it chills, but you may also want to try the Mexican trick of leaving the avocado pit in the soup until serving time.*

Curried Buttermilk and Zucchini Soup

Serves 6 as a first course
Working time: about 30 minutes
Total time: about 1 hour

Calories **95**
Protein **3g.**
Cholesterol **2mg.**
Total fat **5g.**
Saturated fat **1g.**
Sodium **260mg.**

1½ tbsp. safflower oil
1 small onion, chopped
2 garlic cloves, finely chopped
1½ tbsp. finely chopped fresh ginger
½ tsp. ground coriander
½ tsp. ground cumin
½ tsp. turmeric
1½ lb. zucchini, thickly sliced
1 small apple, peeled, cored and sliced
3 cups unsalted chicken stock
½ tsp. salt
1 tbsp. fresh lemon juice
1 cup buttermilk
1 tbsp. finely cut fresh chives

Heat the oil in a large, heavy-bottomed pot over medium-high heat. Add the onion and sauté it, stirring often, until it is translucent — about five minutes. Stir in the garlic, ginger, coriander, cumin and turmeric; sauté the mixture, stirring constantly, for one minute. Add the zucchini and apple, and cook the mixture for one minute more. Pour in the stock and add the salt. Bring the mixture to a boil, then reduce the heat and simmer the soup, partially covered, for 30 minutes.

Purée the soup in several batches in a blender or food processor. Return the soup to the pot; whisk in the lemon juice and buttermilk. Cook the mixture over medium heat until it is heated through — two to three minutes. Garnish the soup with the chives before serving.

Leek, Celery and Gruyère Soup

Serves 4 as a first course
Working time: about 30 minutes
Total time: about 1 hour and 15 minutes

Calories **245**
Protein **13g.**
Cholesterol **27mg.**
Total fat **9g.**
Saturated fat **5g.**
Sodium **400mg.**

4 cups unsalted chicken stock
1 leek, trimmed, all but 1 inch of the green tops discarded, split, washed thoroughly to remove all grit, and chopped (about 2 cups)
7 celery stalks, chopped (about 3 cups), several whole leaves reserved for garnish
½ tsp. fresh lemon juice
2 boiling potatoes, peeled and diced (about 2 cups)
¼ tsp. salt
2 garlic cloves, peeled
7 or 8 drops hot red-pepper sauce
½ tsp. white pepper
½ cup low-fat milk
½ cup shredded Gruyère cheese (about 3 oz.)

Heat ½ cup of the stock in a large, heavy-bottomed pot over medium heat. Add the leek, chopped celery and lemon juice, and cook the mixture until the leek is translucent — about five minutes. Add the potatoes and cook the mixture for seven minutes more, stirring often. Pour in the remaining stock, then add the salt and bring the liquid to a boil. Reduce the heat; add the garlic cloves and simmer the mixture, partially covered, for 30 minutes.

Purée the soup in a blender, food processor or food mill, and return it to the pot. Add the red-pepper sauce, and bring the soup to a simmer. Remove the pot from the heat and season the soup with the white pepper. Whisk in the milk and ¼ cup of the cheese, stirring until the cheese is smoothly incorporated — about two minutes. Garnish the soup with the remaining ¼ cup of the cheese and the reserved celery leaves and serve immediately.

Puréeing: Why and How

Producing perfectly smooth soup — or a velvety base for stew — requires that ingredients be puréed. The means to this end are varied: Where more than one method will do, the preferred one is given first.

For filtering fibrous particles from a dish made with such foods as celery or asparagus, a food mill works best; one with interchangeable plates offers a choice in the texture of the purée. Slower but still effective is the combination of sieve and spoon. Set a sieve over a bowl, then press small batches of the food through the wire mesh with the back of a wooden spoon.

For their speed and efficacy, the blender and food processor are clear favorites. Because the blender yields the smoother purée, such soups as gazpacho, where a coarse texture is the goal, are best prepared in the food processor. For the smoothest texture, purées formed with either device can be sieved.

Tomato Purée with Yogurt-Ricotta Stars

Serves 6 as a first course
Working time: about 25 minutes
Total time: about 45 minutes

Calories **95**
Protein **4g.**
Cholesterol **5mg.**
Total fat **4g.**
Saturated fat **1g.**
Sodium **155mg.**

1 tbsp. virgin olive oil
3 onions, chopped (about 2½ cups)
1 carrot, thinly sliced
1 tsp. chopped fresh thyme, or ¼ tsp. dried thyme leaves
3 garlic cloves, chopped
freshly ground black pepper
28 oz. canned unsalted tomatoes, seeded and coarsely chopped, with their juice
1¼ cups unsalted chicken or vegetable stock
¼ tsp. salt
⅓ cup part-skim ricotta cheese
2 tbsp. plain low-fat yogurt
1½ cups watercress sprigs, stems trimmed

Heat the oil in a large, heavy-bottomed pot over medium heat. Add the onions, carrot, thyme, garlic and some pepper, and cook the mixture, stirring it often, until the onions are translucent — seven to 10 minutes. Add the tomatoes and their juice, the stock and the salt. Reduce the heat and simmer the vegetables for 30 minutes.

While the soup is cooking, purée the cheese and yogurt together in a food processor, blender or food mill. Set the purée aside.

Now purée the soup in batches, processing each batch for about one minute. Return the puréed soup to the pot, bring it to a simmer over medium heat and add the watercress. Simmer the soup just long enough to wilt the watercress — about one minute — then ladle the soup into warmed serving bowls.

Gently spoon 1 heaping tablespoon of the ricotta-yogurt mixture into the middle of each bowl. With the tip of a knife, make a star pattern by pushing a little of the mixture out from the center in several directions. Serve the soup at once.

Scallion Soup

COOKED SCALLIONS HAVE THE MILDNESS
AND SWEETNESS OF LEEKS.

Serves 8 as a first course
Working time: about 15 minutes
Total time: about 50 minutes

Calories **75**
Protein **4g.**
Cholesterol **2mg.**
Total fat **3g.**
Saturated fat **1g.**
Sodium **150mg.**

1 tbsp. virgin olive oil
4 bunches scallions, trimmed, white parts cut into 1-inch lengths, green parts sliced into ¼-inch pieces
8 cups unsalted chicken stock
1 tarragon sprig, leaves stripped and chopped, stem reserved, or 2 tsp. dried tarragon
¼ tsp. salt
freshly ground black pepper

In a large, heavy-bottomed pot, heat the oil over medium-high heat. Add the white parts of the scallions and sauté them until they are soft — about two minutes. Then pour in the stock and add the tarragon stem or 1 teaspoon of the dried tarragon, the salt and some pepper. Reduce the heat and cook the mixture at a strong simmer, uncovered, for 30 minutes. If you used a tarragon stem, remove and discard it.

Add to the pot the tarragon leaves or the remaining teaspoon of dried tarragon, and the green parts of the scallions. Cook the soup until the scallion greens are tender — about four minutes more. Serve at once.

Tarragon-Zucchini Soup

Serves 8 as a first course
Working time: about 50 minutes
Total time: about 1 hour and 10 minutes

Calories **110**
Protein **5g.**
Cholesterol **7mg.**
Total fat **5g.**
Saturated fat **2g.**
Sodium **230mg.**

1 tbsp. unsalted butter
1 tbsp. safflower oil
3 onions, chopped
1½ lb. zucchini, trimmed and cut into 1-inch pieces
2 carrots, thinly sliced
6 cups unsalted chicken stock
1½ tbsp. finely chopped fresh tarragon, plus several tarragon stems tied in a bundle
1 cup low-fat milk
½ tsp. salt
freshly ground black pepper
pinch of cayenne pepper

Melt the butter with the safflower oil in a large, heavy-bottomed pot over medium heat. Add the onions and cook them, stirring often, until they are golden — 15 to 20 minutes. Add the zucchini, carrots, chicken stock and tarragon stems, and bring the mixture to a boil. Reduce the heat, cover the pot, and simmer the liquid for 15 minutes. Remove the lid, increase the heat, and boil the soup, skimming off any impurities that rise to the surface. Continue to cook, stirring occasionally, until the soup is reduced by about one third — 20 to 25 minutes.

Remove the pot from the heat and discard the bundle of tarragon stems. Pour the soup into a large bowl. Purée about two thirds of the soup in a blender or food processor. Return the purée to the pot. Briefly process the remaining third of the soup to achieve a coarse consistency, and pour it back into the pot. Stir in the milk, salt, black pepper and cayenne pepper. Reheat the soup gently without letting it come to a boil. Stir in the chopped tarragon. Serve the soup either warm or chilled.

Black-Eyed Pea and Collard Green Soup

Serves 6
Working time: about 45 minutes
Total time: about 2 hours and 30 minutes
(includes soaking time)

Calories **130**
Protein **8g.**
Cholesterol **5mg.**
Total fat **5g.**
Saturated fat **1g.**
Sodium **500mg.**

1 cup dried black-eyed peas, picked over
1 tbsp. safflower oil
¾ cup chopped onion
1 oz. Canadian bacon, cut into ¼-inch dice
1 garlic clove, finely chopped
1 bay leaf
¼ tsp. hot red-pepper flakes, crushed
5 cups unsalted brown or chicken stock
8 oz. collard greens, trimmed, washed and coarsely chopped (about 4 cups)
1 tsp. salt
2 tsp. cider vinegar

Rinse the peas under cold running water, then put them into a large, heavy pot and pour in enough cold water to cover them by about 3 inches. Discard any peas that float to the surface. Cover the pot, leaving the lid ajar, and slowly bring the liquid to a boil over medium-low heat. Boil the peas for two minutes, then turn off the heat, cover the pot, and let the peas soak for at least one hour. (Alternatively, soak the peas in cold water overnight.)

Heat the oil in a large, heavy-bottomed pot over medium heat. Add the onion and sauté it, stirring occasionally, until it is translucent — about four minutes. Add the bacon and garlic, and cook them for two minutes, stirring frequently.

Drain the peas and add them to the pot along with the bay leaf, red-pepper flakes and stock. Bring the liquid to a boil, then reduce the heat to maintain a simmer, and partially cover the pot. Cook the mixture for 30 minutes, stirring gently several times. Toss in the collard greens and the salt, and cook until the greens are soft and the peas are tender — about 20 minutes. Remove and discard the bay leaf. Stir in the vinegar and serve the soup immediately.

EDITOR'S NOTE: *Mustard greens or kale may be substituted for the collard greens; either of these vegetables will require less cooking than the collard greens.*

Green Pea Soup
with Smoked Salmon

Serves 4
Working time: about 20 minutes
Total time: about 1 hour and 20 minutes

Calories **245**
Protein **9g.**
Cholesterol **9mg.**
Total fat **3g.**
Saturated fat **1g.**
Sodium **160mg.**

1 leek, trimmed, split, thoroughly washed to remove all grit, and sliced
1 onion, sliced
1 carrot, sliced
1 celery stalk, sliced
12 black peppercorns
½ tsp. dill seeds
2 cups frozen green peas (about 10 oz.)
1 cup unsalted chicken stock
2 oz. smoked salmon, cut into small cubes
2 tbsp. light cream
2 tbsp. finely cut fresh dill

Pour 4 cups of water into a large pot; add the leek, onion, carrot, celery, peppercorns and dill seeds. Slowly bring the liquid to a boil, then reduce the heat, and simmer the vegetables for one hour. Add the peas, return the liquid to a simmer, and cook the vegetables for three minutes more.

Purée the contents of the pot in a blender, food processor or food mill. Rinse the pot and return the purée to it; stir in the chicken stock, the salmon and the cream. Bring the soup just to a boil; ladle it into individual soup bowls and garnish each portion with the dill. Serve immediately.

EDITOR'S NOTE: *This soup may be prepared a day in advance and refrigerated covered. If the soup thickens during refrigeration, stir in an additional cup of chicken stock before you reheat the soup.*

Beet and Parsnip Soup

Serves 8 as a first course
Working time: about 30 minutes
Total time: about 50 minutes

Calories **120**
Protein **3g.**
Cholesterol **5mg.**
Total fat **3g.**
Saturated fat **2g.**
Sodium **150mg.**

2 cups unsalted veal, vegetable or chicken stock
1 lb. beets, peeled and coarsely grated
8 oz. parsnips, peeled and coarsely grated
2 tbsp. sugar
1 large, ripe tomato, peeled and seeded
1 apple, peeled, quartered and cored
2 tbsp. fresh lemon juice
2 large onions, finely chopped or grated
1 tbsp. red wine vinegar or white wine vinegar
1 tbsp. finely cut fresh dill, or 1 tsp. dried dillweed
¼ tsp. salt
freshly ground black pepper
½ cup sour cream for garnish

Pour the stock and 3 cups of water into a large pot and bring the liquid to a boil. Add the beets, parsnips and sugar. Reduce the heat, partially cover the pot and simmer the mixture for 20 minutes.

Purée the tomato and the apple in a food processor or blender, then add the purée to the simmering soup. Add the lemon juice, onions and vinegar. Cover the pot and simmer the soup for 20 minutes more. Stir in the dill, salt and some pepper. Serve the soup piping hot, garnished with the sour cream.

Vegetable-Broth Minestrone

Serves 6
Working time: about 30 minutes
Total time: about 2 hours

Calories **305**
Protein **16g.**
Cholesterol **0mg.**
Total fat **2g.**
Saturated fat **0g.**
Sodium **205mg.**

1 cup dried pinto beans, picked over
2 onions, unpeeled, halved crosswise
½ cup dry white wine
8 oz. mushrooms, wiped clean, stems removed and reserved, the caps sliced
1 lb. ripe tomatoes, peeled, seeded and chopped, the peels, seeds and juice reserved, or 14 oz. canned unsalted tomatoes, seeded and chopped, the seeds and juice reserved
2 carrots, sliced
2 celery stalks, sliced, leaves chopped and reserved

1 cauliflower, broken into florets, the leaves and core coarsely chopped and reserved
2 broccoli stalks, the florets broken off (about 2 cups), the leaves and stalks coarsely chopped and reserved
1 whole garlic bulb, the unpeeled cloves separated and crushed with the side of a heavy knife, plus 4 garlic cloves, chopped
24 black peppercorns
1 tsp. fresh rosemary, or ¼ tsp. dried rosemary
2 bay leaves
2 lemon-zest strips, each about 2 inches long
4 oz. ziti or other tubular pasta
juice of ½ lemon
¼ tsp. salt
1 cup sliced fresh basil leaves, or ¼ cup chopped fresh parsley
freshly ground black pepper
½ cup freshly grated Parmesan cheese

Rinse the beans under cold running water. Put the beans into a large pot and pour in enough cold water to cover them by about 3 inches. Discard any beans that float to the surface. Boil the beans for two minutes, then turn off the heat, cover the pot, and soak the beans for at least an hour. (Alternatively, soak the beans overnight in cold water.)

At the end of the soaking time, pour in enough additional water to cover the beans by about 3 inches. Bring the liquid to a boil, reduce the heat to maintain a strong simmer, and cook the beans until they are tender — about 30 minutes. Then drain the beans and set them aside.

While the beans are simmering, start the vegetable broth. Heat a large, heavy-bottomed pot over medium-high heat and place the onions flat sides down in the pot. Cook the onions until their cut surfaces turn dark brown — about 10 minutes. (The onions will help to color the stock.) Pour in the wine, stirring with a wooden spoon to dislodge the onions and dissolve their caramelized juices. Add the mushroom stems, the tomato peels, seeds and juice, half of the carrots, the sliced celery, the chopped cauliflower leaves and cores, the chopped broccoli leaves and stalks, the crushed garlic cloves, peppercorns, rosemary, bay leaves, lemon zest and 12 cups of water. Bring the liquid to a boil, then reduce the heat to maintain a simmer and cook the broth for one hour.

While the broth is simmering, add the ziti to 6 cups of boiling water with 1 teaspoon of salt. Start testing the pasta after eight minutes and cook it until it is *al dente*. Drain the pasta, rinse it under cold running water to keep it from sticking together, and set it aside.

In a small bowl, mix the chopped tomato and the chopped garlic with the lemon juice and salt, and set the mixture aside.

When the vegetable broth has simmered for one hour, strain it into a bowl and discard the solids. Rinse the pot and return the strained broth to it. Bring the broth to a boil. Reduce the heat to medium, then add the sliced mushroom caps and the remaining carrots, and simmer them for four minutes. Add the cauliflower florets and simmer them for four minutes more. Add the broccoli florets, celery leaves and beans, and simmer them for an additional three minutes.

Transfer the drained ziti to the pot and cook for two minutes to warm the pasta through. Stir in the tomato-garlic mixture and the basil or parsley. Season the minestrone with a generous grinding of pepper, and serve it with the grated cheese alongside.

Gazpacho Blanco

Serves 4 as a first course
Working time: about 10 minutes
Total time: about 40 minutes

Calories **165**
Protein **7g.**
Cholesterol **7mg.**
Total fat **2g.**
Saturated fat **1g.**
Sodium **220mg.**

1 lb. seedless white grapes
3 cucumbers
1 shallot, sliced
1 small garlic clove, finely chopped
¼ tsp. salt
¼ tsp. white pepper
2 cups plain low-fat yogurt
5 to 8 drops hot red-pepper sauce

Wash and stem the grapes. Cut several grapes in half lengthwise and set them aside. Purée the remaining grapes in a food processor or blender. Strain the purée through a sieve and return it to the food processor or blender.

Cut several very thin slices from the center of a cucumber and set them aside. Peel the cucumbers, halve them lengthwise, and seed them. Cut the cucumbers into thick slices and add them to the grape purée in the processor or blender. Add the shallot, garlic, salt and pepper, and briefly process the mixture until the cucumbers are reduced to fine pieces.

Pour the mixture into a chilled serving bowl and whisk in the yogurt and red-pepper sauce. Cover the soup and refrigerate it until it is well chilled — about 30 minutes. Serve the soup in chilled bowls, garnished with the reserved cucumber slices and grape halves.

Onion and Red Potato Soup with Walnut Toasts

Serves 4 as a first course
Working (and total) time: about 30 minutes

Calories **220**
Protein **7g.**
Cholesterol **2mg.**
Total fat **9g.**
Saturated fat **1g.**
Sodium **290mg.**

4 cups unsalted chicken stock
2 onions (about 10 oz.), cut into eighths
8 oz. red potatoes, unpeeled, cut into ¾-inch pieces
¼ tsp. salt
freshly ground black pepper
4 garlic cloves, finely chopped
¼ cup coarsely chopped walnuts, plus 4 large walnut halves
4 French-bread slices, each about ¼ inch thick
¼ cup thinly sliced fresh basil leaves

Pour the stock into a large saucepan over medium heat. When the stock begins to steam, add the onions, potatoes, salt, some pepper and half of the garlic. Simmer the liquid until the potatoes can be easily pierced with a fork — 10 to 15 minutes.

While the potatoes are cooking, preheat the oven to 400° F. Using a mortar and pestle, crush 3 tablespoons of the walnuts with the remaining garlic to form a paste. Spread one fourth of the paste on each slice of bread, then press a walnut half into the center of each slice. Toast the bread in the oven until the slices are slightly browned on the bottom — about five minutes.

Stir the basil into the soup and immediately ladle the soup into four heated bowls. Float a walnut-covered slice of bread in the center of each bowl; sprinkle some of the remaining chopped walnuts around each slice and serve the soup immediately.

Cold Curried Vegetable Soup

Serves 4 as a first course
Working time: about 20 minutes
Total time: about 2 hours and 20 minutes
(includes chilling)

Calories **130**
Protein **5g.**
Cholesterol **1mg.**
Total fat **4g.**
Saturated fat **1g.**
Sodium **220mg.**

2 tsp. safflower oil
1 small onion, thinly sliced
2 tbsp. mild curry powder
2 garlic cloves, finely chopped
14 oz. canned unsalted tomatoes, coarsely chopped, with their juice
3 cups unsalted chicken stock
1 tsp. chopped fresh thyme, or ¼ tsp. dried thyme leaves
1 green pepper, seeded, deribbed and cut into ½-inch pieces
1 cup cauliflower florets, thinly sliced lengthwise
1 small carrot, thinly sliced
1 small zucchini, thinly sliced
1 small yellow squash, halved lengthwise and thinly sliced across
1 tbsp. balsamic vinegar or red wine vinegar
¼ tsp. salt
freshly ground black pepper

Heat the safflower oil in a large, heavy-bottomed saucepan over medium heat. Add the onion slices and sauté them, stirring, until they are translucent — about four minutes. Sprinkle in the curry powder and cook the mixture, stirring constantly, for one minute. Add the garlic and cook it for 30 seconds. Stir in the tomatoes with their juice and cook them, stirring frequently, until the liquid is reduced by about one third — 10 to 15 minutes.

While the tomatoes are cooking, pour the stock into a pot over medium-high heat. Add the thyme and place a steamer in the pot. Arrange the green pepper, cauliflower, carrot, zucchini and squash in the steamer. Cover the pot and steam the vegetables until they are tender — five to seven minutes. Transfer the vegetables to the tomato mixture and pour in the steaming liquid. Add the vinegar, salt and some black pepper, then gently stir the soup to incorporate the vegetables. Refrigerate the soup, partially covered, for at least two hours before serving.

EDITOR'S NOTE: *This soup may be prepared as much as two days in advance.*

Cold Parsley Soup with Icy Tomato Granita

GRANITA IS THE ITALIAN NAME FOR A WATER ICE.
THE CRYSTALLINE TEXTURE OF THE TOMATO-MINT GRANITA
USED HERE PROVIDES A SUBTLE COUNTERPOINT TO THE
SOUP'S SMOOTHNESS.

Serves 6 as a first course
Working time: about 45 minutes
Total time: about 3 hours and 45 minutes
(includes chilling)

Calories **100**
Protein **4g.**
Cholesterol **1mg.**
Total fat **4g.**
Saturated fat **1g.**
Sodium **255mg.**

1 tbsp. virgin olive oil
4 scallions, trimmed and thinly sliced
1 onion, thinly sliced
2 garlic cloves, finely chopped
¼ tsp. salt
freshly ground black pepper
4 cups unsalted chicken or vegetable stock
1 potato, peeled and thinly sliced
4 cups parsley leaves, preferably Italian
6 mint sprigs for garnish
Tomato granita
1 lb. ripe tomatoes, peeled, cored and quartered
¼ tsp. salt
1 tbsp. fresh lemon juice
2 tbsp. finely chopped fresh mint

To prepare the granita, purée the tomatoes in a blender or food processor, then strain the purée through a sieve into a bowl. Stir in the salt, lemon juice and mint. Pour the mixture into ice-cube trays and freeze it for two to three hours.

Meanwhile, heat the oil in a large, heavy-bottomed pot over medium heat. Add the scallions, onion, garlic, salt and some pepper. Cook the mixture, stirring often, until the onion is translucent — about five minutes. Pour in the stock, then add the potato slices. Reduce the heat, cover the pot, and simmer the liquid until a potato slice can be easily crushed with the back of a fork — 25 to 30 minutes.

While the stock is simmering, bring a large pot of water to a boil. Add the parsley leaves; as soon as the water returns to a boil, drain the leaves and refresh them under cold running water.

Purée the parsley and the stock-vegetable mixture together in a blender or food processor. Strain the purée through a sieve into a bowl and let it cool to room temperature. Cover the bowl with plastic wrap and refrigerate it until the soup is thoroughly chilled — at least two hours.

Purée the cubes of granita in a food processor just until the mixture is grainy. Transfer the cold parsley soup to six chilled soup bowls. Spoon some of the granita into each bowl; garnish with the mint sprigs and serve immediately.

Corn and Cilantro Soup

Serves 4 as a first course
Working (and total) time: about 20 minutes

Calories **160**
Protein **5g.**
Cholesterol **6mg.**
Total fat **5g.**
Saturated fat **2g.**
Sodium **330mg.**

2 tsp. unsalted butter
1 tsp. safflower oil
1 onion, finely chopped
3 garlic cloves, finely chopped
1 tsp. cumin seeds, ground with a mortar and pestle, or 1 tsp. ground cumin (optional)
1 green pepper, seeded, deribbed and chopped
1 sweet red pepper, seeded, deribbed and chopped
1 jalapeño pepper (optional), seeded and finely chopped (caution, page 95)
1 ripe tomato, peeled, seeded and chopped
2 cups fresh or frozen corn kernels
2 cups unsalted chicken stock
½ tsp. salt
2 tbsp. chopped cilantro

Heat the butter and the oil together in a large, heavy-bottomed saucepan or skillet over medium heat. Add the onion, garlic and, if you are using it, the cumin. Cook, stirring often, until the onion is translucent — about five minutes. Stir in all the peppers and cook them until they soften slightly — about two minutes

more. Add the tomato, corn, stock and salt. Reduce the heat and simmer the soup for five minutes. Stir in the cilantro just before serving.

Cabbage and Caraway Soup

Serves 10 as a first course
Working time: about 45 minutes
Total time: about 1 hour and 45 minutes

Calories **75**
Protein **3g.**
Cholesterol **1mg.**
Total fat **4g.**
Saturated fat **0g.**
Sodium **165mg.**

2 tbsp. safflower oil
one 3-lb. cabbage, cored, quartered and thinly sliced
1½ tsp. caraway seeds
1 tsp. mustard seeds
½ tsp. salt
¼ cup red wine vinegar or white wine vinegar
4 cups unsalted chicken or veal stock
4 garlic cloves, finely chopped
14 oz. canned unsalted tomatoes, puréed with their juice
¼ to ½ tsp. cayenne pepper
2 tbsp. finely cut fresh dill, or 1 tbsp. dried dillweed

Heat the safflower oil in a large, heavy-bottomed pot over medium heat. Add the cabbage, caraway seeds, mustard seeds and salt. Cover the pot, and cook, stirring occasionally, until the cabbage is wilted — about 25 minutes.

Add the vinegar and cook the mixture, stirring, for one minute. Pour in the stock and 3 cups of cold water, then stir in the garlic, the tomato purée and the cayenne pepper. Reduce the heat and slowly bring the liquid to a simmer. Cook the soup gently for 45 minutes. Stir in the dill and serve immediately.

Hot and Sour Soup

THE LILY BUDS CALLED FOR HERE ARE THE DRIED BUDS
OF COMMON DAY LILIES. AVAILABLE AT ASIAN MARKETS, THEY
ADD UNUSUAL TEXTURE AND FLAVOR TO THE SOUP.

Serves 8 as a first course
Working (and total) time: about 30 minutes

Calories **80**
Protein **5g.**
Cholesterol **1mg.**
Total fat **2g.**
Saturated fat **0g.**
Sodium **190mg.**

6 cups unsalted chicken stock
¼ cup rice vinegar
2 tbsp. Chinese black vinegar or balsamic vinegar
1 to 2 tsp. chili paste with garlic, or 5 to 10 drops hot red-pepper sauce
1 tbsp. low-sodium soy sauce
1 tbsp. dry sherry
½ tsp. finely chopped garlic
1 to 2 tsp. finely chopped fresh ginger
1 carrot, julienned
6 dried shiitake or Chinese black mushrooms, covered with boiling water and soaked for 20 minutes, stemmed, the caps thinly sliced
¼ cup cloud-ear mushrooms (optional), covered with boiling water and soaked for 20 minutes, thinly sliced
16 lily buds (optional), covered with boiling water and soaked for 5 minutes, trimmed, each bud tied in a knot
¾ cup bamboo shoots (optional), rinsed and julienned
2 tbsp. cornstarch, mixed with 3 tbsp. water
8 oz. firm bean curd (tofu), cut into thin strips
3 scallions, trimmed and sliced diagonally into ovals

Heat the stock in a large pot over medium-high heat. Add the vinegars, chili paste or hot red-pepper sauce, soy sauce, sherry, garlic, ginger, carrot and shiitake or Chinese black mushrooms, and, if you are using them, the cloud-ear mushrooms, lily buds and bamboo shoots. Bring the liquid to a boil, then stir in the cornstarch mixture. Reduce the heat and simmer the soup, stirring, until it thickens slightly — two to three minutes. Gently stir in the bean curd. Ladle the soup into bowls and garnish each serving with the scallion slices.

Puréed Cauliflower Soup

Serves 8
Working time: about 45 minutes
Total time: about 1 hour

Calories **125**
Protein **7g.**
Cholesterol **15mg.**
Total fat **6g.**
Saturated fat **3g.**
Sodium **230mg.**

1 tbsp. unsalted butter
3 onions (about 1 lb.), thinly sliced
2 tsp. fresh thyme, or ½ tsp. dried thyme leaves
1 large cauliflower (about 2 lb.), cored, the florets cut off
7 garlic cloves, thinly sliced
6 cups unsalted chicken stock
½ tsp. salt
½ tsp. grated nutmeg
freshly ground black pepper
½ cup part-skim ricotta cheese
2 tbsp. plain low-fat yogurt
¼ cup light cream
1 tsp. turmeric

Melt the butter in a large, heavy-bottomed pot over medium heat; then stir in the sliced onions and the thyme. Cover the pot and cook the onions, stirring frequently to keep them from browning, until they become very soft — about 15 minutes.

Reserve 1 cup of the smallest cauliflower florets and set them aside for the garnish. Stir the remaining cauliflower florets and the garlic into the onion mixture. Cover the pot and cook the cauliflower for 15 minutes, stirring occasionally to prevent burning. Add the stock, salt, nutmeg and some pepper; simmer the mixture, covered, until the cauliflower is soft — about 20 minutes.

While the cauliflower is cooking, put the cheese and yogurt in a blender or food processor, and purée the mixture until it is very smooth. Transfer the mixture to a bowl, then whisk in the cream.

When the cauliflower is soft, purée the mixture in a blender or food processor in several batches. Return the batches of purée to the pot and keep it warm over low heat. Whisk in the cheese-yogurt mixture.

To prepare the garnish, combine the reserved cauliflower florets in a small skillet with the turmeric and just enough water to cover the florets. Bring the water to a boil, reduce the heat, and simmer the florets until they are tender — about seven minutes. Gently place several yellow florets on top of each portion of soup and serve at once.

Cauliflower Soup
Provençale

Serves 6 as a first course
Working time: about 15 minutes
Total time: about 40 minutes

Calories **105**
Protein **5g.**
Cholesterol **6mg.**
Total fat **3g.**
Saturated fat **1g.**
Sodium **145mg.**

1 cauliflower (about 1½ lb.), cut into small florets, stems discarded
3 cups unsalted chicken stock
2 ripe tomatoes, peeled, seeded and chopped
1 cup chopped onion
4 garlic cloves, finely chopped
1 tsp. dried basil
½ cup dry white wine
¼ tsp. salt
freshly ground black pepper
2 tbsp. cut fresh dill or chopped fresh basil or Italian parsley
1 tbsp. unsalted butter

Blanch the cauliflower florets in 2 quarts of boiling water for one minute. Drain the florets in a colander and set them aside.

Pour the stock into a large pot. Add the tomatoes, onion, garlic, dried basil, wine, salt and some pepper, and bring the liquid to a boil. Reduce the heat and simmer the mixture for 10 minutes, stirring once.

Add the cauliflower and simmer the soup until the florets are tender — 10 to 15 minutes. Reduce the heat and let the soup simmer for 10 minutes to meld the flavors. Stir in the dill or other fresh herbs and the butter. Serve immediately.

Curried Yellow Split Pea Soup with Lamb and Mint

Serves 4
Working time: about 30 minutes
Total time: about 2 hours and 30 minutes

Calories **325**
Protein **20g.**
Cholesterol **23mg.**
Total fat **10g.**
Saturated fat **1g.**
Sodium **460mg.**

6 oz. dried yellow split peas (about ¾ cup), picked over and rinsed
1 tbsp. safflower oil
1 lamb shank (about 12 oz.), trimmed of fat
1 onion, coarsely chopped
¼ cup thinly sliced celery
2 tbsp. curry powder
2 garlic cloves, finely chopped
1 small bay leaf
2 tbsp. chopped fresh mint
1 carrot, thinly sliced
1 tsp. salt
¼ tsp. white pepper
juice of half a lemon
4 mint sprigs for garnish

In a large, heavy-bottomed soup pot, heat the safflower oil over medium-high heat and cook the lamb shank until it is brown on all sides — three to five minutes. Reduce the heat to medium and add the onion, celery and curry powder. Cook the vegetables, stirring constantly, until the onion turns translucent — three to five minutes. Add the garlic and continue to cook for 30 seconds, stirring to keep the mixture from burning. Add the peas, the bay leaf and 6 cups of water. Bring the mixture to a boil, skim off any impurities, then add the chopped mint. Partially cover the pan, reduce the heat, and simmer the soup until the meat and the peas are tender — about one hour.

Remove the lamb shank, and when it is cool enough to handle, trim the meat from the bone; cut the meat into bite-size pieces and set them aside. Remove the bay leaf from the peas and discard it. Purée the peas in a blender or food processor, then return them to the pot. Add the lamb and carrot, and cook, covered, over medium heat until the carrot slices are tender — about five minutes. Season the soup with the salt, some pepper and the lemon juice. Serve in individual bowls, each garnished with a sprig of mint.

Caraway-Flavored Celeriac Soup

Serves 6 as a first course
Working time: about 25 minutes
Total time: about 1 hour

Calories **145**
Protein **5g.**
Cholesterol **7mg.**
Total fat **7g.**
Saturated fat **2g.**
Sodium **315mg.**

1 tbsp. safflower oil
1 tbsp. unsalted butter
2 onions, chopped
1½ lb. celeriac, peeled and cut into ¼-inch cubes
1 carrot, coarsely chopped
8 cups unsalted chicken stock
½ tsp. salt
freshly ground black pepper
½ tsp. caraway seeds
1 tbsp. fresh lemon juice
2 tbsp. chopped fresh parsley

Put 1 cup of the cubed celeriac and 1 cup of the stock into a small saucepan. Bring the mixture to a boil, reduce the heat, and simmer, covered, until the celeriac is tender — about 5 minutes. Set the saucepan aside.

Heat the oil and butter together in a large, heavy-bottomed pot over medium heat. Add the onions and cook them, stirring often, until they are translucent — about 10 minutes. Add the remaining celeriac, carrot and 6 cups of the stock, and bring the liquid to a boil. Reduce the heat to medium, cover the pot and simmer the mixture for 15 minutes. Remove the lid and continue cooking the mixture until it is reduced by one third — about 10 minutes.

Remove the pot from the heat and purée the soup in batches in a blender, food processor or food mill. Return the soup to the pot and pour in the remaining 2 cups of stock along with the reserved celeriac cubes and their cooking liquid. Stir in the salt, pepper, caraway seeds, lemon juice and parsley. Briefly reheat the soup and serve it at once.

EDITOR'S NOTE: *This soup is also excellent served cold with baby shrimp floating on top.*

Escarole Soup with Turnips and Apple

Serves 6 as a first course
Working time: about 20 minutes
Total time: about 50 minutes

Calories **105**
Protein **4g.**
Cholesterol **3mg.**
Total fat **4g.**
Saturated fat **1g.**
Sodium **135mg.**

1 tbsp. virgin olive oil	
1 onion, chopped	
2 medium turnips, chopped	
1 carrot, chopped	
1 tsp. fresh thyme, or ¼ tsp. dried thyme leaves	
¼ tsp. salt	
freshly ground black pepper	
½ cup dry white wine	
1 tbsp. red wine vinegar	
3 cups unsalted chicken stock	
1 tart apple, peeled, cored and chopped	

1 head escarole (about 12 oz.), washed and shredded
grated zest of 1 orange
¼ cup freshly grated Parmesan cheese

Heat the oil in a large, heavy-bottomed pot over medium-high heat. Add the onion, turnips, carrot, thyme, salt and some pepper. Sauté the vegetables, stirring occasionally, until the onion is translucent — about four minutes. Pour in the wine and vinegar, and reduce the heat to medium. Cook the vegetables, covered, for 20 minutes.

Pour in the stock and 3 cups of water, then add the chopped apple. Bring the liquid to a boil; then reduce the heat to maintain a simmer, cover the pot, and cook the soup for five minutes more. Add the escarole and cook it until it is wilted — about 10 minutes. Sprinkle the zest onto the hot soup and serve it immediately, with the cheese alongside.

Peppery Peanut Soup

THIS LIGHT RENDITION OF PEANUT SOUP HAS A SMALL FRACTION
OF THE FAT CONTAINED IN THE TRADITIONAL CREAMY VERSION.

Serves 4
Working time: about 10 minutes
Total time: about 25 minutes

Calories **140**
Protein **6g.**
Cholesterol **17mg.**
Total fat **11g.**
Saturated fat **4g.**
Sodium **265mg.**

2 tsp. unsalted butter
½ cup finely chopped celery
1 garlic clove, finely chopped
1 tbsp. flour
4 cups unsalted chicken stock
¼ cup light cream
2 tbsp. peanut butter
¼ tsp. salt
⅛ to ¼ tsp. crushed hot red-pepper flakes or cayenne pepper
2 scallions, trimmed and sliced diagonally into very thin ovals

Melt the butter in a large, heavy-bottomed pot over medium-low heat. Add the celery and garlic and cook them for two minutes. Stir in the flour and cook the mixture for one minute, stirring constantly. Whisk in the stock, peanut butter, salt and pepper, and simmer the mixture for 15 minutes. Stir in the scallions and the cream, and let the soup heat through before serving.

White Bean Soup Cooked with a Bulb of Garlic

Serves 6
Working time: about 45 minutes
Total time: about 3 hours and 20 minutes
(includes soaking)

Calories **255**
Protein **15g.**
Cholesterol **1mg.**
Total fat **5g.**
Saturated fat **1g.**
Sodium **465mg.**

2 cups dried Great Northern beans, picked over
6 cups unsalted chicken stock
1 onion
1 carrot, halved crosswise
1 celery stalk, halved crosswise
1 leek, trimmed, split and washed thoroughly to remove all grit
1 bay leaf
2 tsp. fresh thyme, or ½ tsp. dried thyme leaves
1 large whole garlic bulb, the papery outer skin removed
1 tsp. salt
1 tbsp. virgin olive oil
3 ripe plum tomatoes, peeled, seeded and chopped (about 1 cup)
½ cup chopped fresh parsley, preferably Italian, plus 1 tbsp. for garnish
freshly ground black pepper

Rinse the beans under cold running water, then put them into a large, heavy-bottomed pot, and pour in enough water to cover them by about 3 inches. Discard any beans that float to the surface. Cover the pot, leaving the lid ajar, and slowly bring the liquid to a boil over medium-low heat. Boil the beans for two minutes, then turn off the heat and soak the beans, covered, for at least one hour. (Alternatively, soak the beans overnight in cold water.)

Drain the beans in a colander and return them to the pot. Pour in the stock, then add the onion, carrot, celery, leek, bay leaf and thyme. Slowly bring the liquid to a boil over medium-low heat. Reduce the heat to maintain a simmer, and cover the pot. Cook the beans, stirring occasionally and skimming any foam from the surface, until they are tender — one to one and a half hours. When the beans have been simmering for 30 minutes, add the whole garlic bulb and the salt.

Near the end of the cooking time, pour the olive oil into a heavy-bottomed skillet over high heat. Add the tomatoes and cook them for three to five minutes, stirring frequently. Then stir in the ½ cup of

chopped parsley and set the skillet aside.

Drain the beans in a sieve set over a large bowl to catch the cooking liquid. Discard all the vegetables but the garlic. Return two thirds of the cooked beans to the pot. When the garlic bulb is cool enough to handle, separate it into its individual cloves and slip off their skins. Purée the garlic and the remaining beans in a food processor or food mill along with 1 cup of the reserved cooking liquid. (Alternatively, press the garlic

and beans through a sieve with a wooden spoon, then stir in 1 cup of the reserved cooking liquid.)

Transfer the garlic-bean purée to the pot with the beans and carefully stir in the remaining cooking liquid. Reheat the soup over low heat, then fold in the tomato mixture. Cook the soup for one or two minutes more. Season the soup with some pepper and serve it immediately, with the remaining tablespoon of parsley sprinkled over the top.

Chestnut Soup

Serves 4
Working time: about 20 minutes
Total time: about 1 hour and 10 minutes

Calories **380**
Protein **8g.**
Cholesterol **6mg.**
Total fat **9g.**
Saturated fat **2g.**
Sodium **220mg.**

1¼ lb. fresh chestnuts
2 tsp. safflower oil
1 leek, trimmed, the green tops discarded, the stalks split, washed thoroughly to remove all grit, and cut into ½-inch pieces
½ cup dry sherry
4 oz. mushrooms, stemmed, the caps thinly sliced
2 to 3 cups unsalted chicken stock
¼ tsp. salt
¼ tsp. white pepper
1 cup low-fat milk
1½ tbsp. sliced toasted almonds

Using a small, sharp knife, cut a shallow cross in the flat side of each chestnut. Drop the chestnuts into 1½ quarts of boiling water and cook them for 10 minutes.

Drain the chestnuts and let them cool slightly; peel them while they are still warm.

Heat the oil in a large, heavy-bottomed pot over medium heat. Add the leek pieces and sauté them, stirring frequently, until they are translucent — four to five minutes. Pour in the sherry, increase the heat to medium high, and cook the mixture until the liquid is reduced by three quarters — three to four minutes. Add the chestnuts, mushrooms and 2 cups of the stock. Bring the liquid to a boil, then reduce the heat and simmer the mixture, covered, until the chestnuts can be easily pierced with the tip of a sharp knife — 25 to 30 minutes.

Purée the mixture in a food processor, blender or food mill. Add the salt and pepper. Pour in the milk in stages, puréeing the mixture after each addition. (If you prefer a thinner soup, incorporate another cup of stock into the purée.)

Return the purée to the pot and reheat it for two to three minutes over medium heat. Garnish with the almonds before serving.

Gazpacho with Roasted Peppers

Serves 4 as a first course
Working time: about 50 minutes
Total time: about 1 hour and 50 minutes

Calories **70**
Protein **2g.**
Cholesterol **0mg.**
Total fat **4g.**
Saturated fat **1g.**
Sodium **170mg.**

1 large sweet red pepper
1 large green pepper
2 ripe tomatoes, peeled, seeded and coarsely chopped
2 celery stalks, thinly sliced
1 cucumber, peeled, halved lengthwise, seeded and cut into large chunks
2 garlic cloves, chopped
1 cup coarsely chopped fresh watercress, plus 4 whole sprigs for garnish
½ cup unsalted veal or vegetable stock
¼ cup fresh orange juice
1 tbsp. fresh lemon juice
1 tbsp. virgin olive oil
¼ tsp. salt
freshly ground black pepper

Preheat the broiler. Broil the peppers 2 to 3 inches below the heat source, turning them often, until they are uniformly blistered and blackened — 12 to 15 minutes. Transfer the peppers to a bowl and tightly cover the bowl with plastic wrap. Let the peppers stand for five minutes — the trapped steam will loosen their skin.

Make a slit in one of the peppers and pour the juices that have collected inside it into the bowl. Peel the pepper from top to bottom. Halve the pepper lengthwise, then remove and discard the stem, seeds and ribs. Repeat the procedure with the other pepper.

Put the peppers and their juices into a food processor or blender along with the tomatoes, celery, cucumber, garlic, chopped watercress, stock, orange juice, lemon juice, oil, salt and some pepper. Process the mixture in short bursts until a coarse purée results. Transfer the gazpacho to a bowl; refrigerate it for at least one hour, then garnish it with the watercress sprigs and serve.

EDITOR'S NOTE: *This soup may be prepared as much as 24 hours in advance.*

Roquefort Onion Soup

Serves 8 as a first course
Working time: about 45 minutes
Total time: about 1 hour and 15 minutes

Calories **200**
Protein **7g.**
Cholesterol **16mg.**
Total fat **9g.**
Saturated fat **4g.**
Sodium **420mg.**

1 tbsp. unsalted butter
1 tbsp. safflower oil
2 lb. onions, thinly sliced
2 garlic cloves, finely chopped
8 cups unsalted chicken or veal stock
2 cups dry white wine
2 tsp. fresh thyme, or ½ tsp. dried thyme leaves
2 tsp. fresh lemon juice
½ tsp. salt
⅛ tsp. cayenne pepper
freshly ground black pepper
4 oz. Roquefort cheese, crumbled
1 tbsp. chopped fresh parsley

Melt the butter and oil in a large, heavy-bottomed pot over medium-low heat. Add the onions and garlic and partially cover the pot. Cook for three minutes, stirring once. Remove the lid and continue cooking, stirring frequently, until the onions are browned — 20 to 35 minutes. Pour in 6 cups of the stock and the wine, then add the thyme. Bring the liquid to a boil, lower the heat and simmer the mixture until it is reduced by one third — about 30 minutes. With a slotted spoon, remove about 1½ cups of the onions and set them aside.

Purée the soup in a blender, food processor or food mill. Return the soup to the pot and stir in the reserved onions. Pour in the remaining 2 cups of stock, then add the lemon juice, salt, cayenne pepper and some black pepper. Reheat the soup over medium heat for two minutes. In the meantime, combine the cheese and parsley in a small bowl and sprinkle the mixture over the soup just before serving.

carrots are soft — eight to 10 minutes.

While the soup is boiling, bring the remaining 1½ cups of stock to a simmer in a small saucepan over medium heat. Add the diced carrots and the raisins and simmer them, covered, until the carrots are tender — about five minutes. Set the saucepan aside.

Purée the soup in batches in a blender, food processor or food mill. Return the soup to the pot over medium heat and add the diced carrots and raisins with their cooking liquid. Stir in the cream, salt, some pepper and the parsley. Simmer the soup until it is heated through — about two minutes — and serve at once.

Cream of Carrot Soup with Fresh Ginger

Serves 8 as a first course
Working time: about 30 minutes
Total time: about 1 hour

Calories **155**
Protein **4g.**
Cholesterol **15mg.**
Total fat **8g.**
Saturated fat **3g.**
Sodium **350mg.**

2 lb. carrots
2 tsp. safflower oil
2 tsp. unsalted butter
2 onions, chopped (about 1½ cups)
¼ cup grated fresh ginger
8 cups unsalted chicken stock
¼ cup golden raisins, chopped
½ cup light cream
¾ tsp. salt
freshly ground black pepper
2 tbsp. chopped fresh parsley

Cut two of the carrots into small dice and set them aside. Slice the remaining carrots into thin rounds.

Heat the oil and butter together in a large, heavy-bottomed pot over medium heat. Add the onions and cook them, stirring occasionally, until they are golden — about 10 minutes. Add the carrot rounds and the ginger, and stir in 1½ cups of the stock. Reduce the heat, cover the pot, and cook the mixture until the carrots are tender — about 20 minutes.

Pour 5 cups of the remaining stock into the pot and bring the liquid to a boil. Reduce the heat, cover the pot, and simmer the stock for 10 minutes. Remove the lid and increase the heat to high. Boil the soup, skimming the impurities from the surface several times, until the liquid is reduced by about one third and the

Chilled Curried Cucumber Soup

Serves 6 as a first course
Working time: about 20 minutes
Total time: about 1 hour and 20 minutes (includes chilling)

Calories **95**
Protein **5g.**
Cholesterol **10mg.**
Total fat **5g.**
Saturated fat **3g.**
Sodium **165mg.**

1 cup loosely packed cilantro, a few leaves reserved for garnish
1 onion, quartered
2 large cucumbers, peeled, quartered lengthwise, seeded and cut into chunks
½ cup sour cream
1½ cups plain low-fat yogurt
1 tsp. curry powder
¼ tsp. salt
¼ tsp. white pepper
3 to 5 drops hot red-pepper sauce
1¼ cups unsalted brown or chicken stock

Chop the cilantro in a food processor. Add the onion and cucumber chunks, and process them until they are finely chopped but not puréed. (Alternatively, chop the cilantro by hand and grate or finely chop the onion and cucumbers.)

In a bowl, whisk the sour cream with 1 cup of the yogurt, the curry powder, salt, white pepper and red-pepper sauce. Whisk in the cucumber mixture and the stock. Refrigerate the soup for at least one hour. Serve the soup in chilled bowls; garnish each portion with a dollop of the remaining yogurt and the reserved cilantro leaves.

EDITOR'S NOTE: *This soup is even better when it is made a day in advance.*

Turnip Soup

Serves 4 as a first course
Working time: about 45 minutes
Total time: about 1 hour

Calories **130**	
Protein **4g.**	*1½ tbsp. unsalted butter*
Cholesterol **13mg.**	*1 lb. small white turnips, peeled, quartered and thinly sliced crosswise*
Total fat **6g.**	*¼ tsp. salt*
Saturated fat **3g.**	*¼ tsp. grated nutmeg*
Sodium **250mg.**	*3 cups unsalted chicken stock*
	3 small boiling potatoes
	2 tbsp. loosely packed fresh chervil leaves or chopped fresh parsley

Melt the butter in a large, heavy-bottomed pot over medium heat. Stir in the turnips and cook them, stir-ring frequently, until they are golden brown — approximately 20 minutes.

Season the turnips with the salt and nutmeg, and toss them gently. Remove and reserve ½ cup of the turnips to use as a garnish.

Pour the stock into the pot; then cover it and bring the liquid to a boil. Reduce the heat and simmer the soup for 20 minutes, skimming off any foam that rises to the surface.

At the end of the 20 minutes, peel and quarter the potatoes, then cut them crosswise into thin slices and add them to the soup. Simmer the soup until the potatoes are tender but still intact — 10 to 15 minutes. Taste the soup for seasoning and add more nutmeg if necessary. Garnish the soup with the chervil or parsley and the reserved turnips before serving.

Consommé

Serves 6 as a first course
Working time: about 30 minutes
Total time: about 1 hour

Calories **30**
Protein **3g.**
Cholesterol **0mg.**
Total fat **0g.**
Saturated fat **0g.**
Sodium **270mg.**

8 cups unsalted brown, veal or chicken stock, thoroughly degreased (box, page 55)
3 egg whites
4 oz. lean beef, veal or chicken, trimmed of all fat and finely chopped
1 carrot, finely chopped
1 celery stalk, finely chopped
1 leek, trimmed, split and washed thoroughly to remove all grit, thinly sliced, or 1 onion, finely chopped
1 sprig thyme, or ¼ tsp. dried thyme leaves
1 bay leaf
3 parsley sprigs, chopped
freshly ground black pepper
½ tsp. salt

Pour the stock into a 4-quart pot and bring the liquid to a boil. While the stock is coming to a boil, put the egg whites into a bowl and beat them lightly. Stir the remaining ingredients into the egg whites.

Add the contents of the bowl to the boiling stock all at one time. Stir the mixture once or twice, and then stop stirring. Adjust the heat to maintain a slow simmer; do not allow the mixture to boil vigorously. The clarification ingredients should rise to the surface, forming a "raft," which will act as a filter. A hole or fissure should form in the raft; using a ladle or a spoon, gently enlarge the opening so that the stock can bubble up through it and over the filter. Simmer the consommé for 30 minutes.

Place a sieve or colander over a clean bowl and line it with several layers of cheesecloth or a clean dish towel. When the consommé is done, ladle it from the hole in the raft, being careful not to break the raft, and strain it through the sieve into the bowl.

EDITOR'S NOTE: *Consommé is clarified stock. Although the egg whites are essential to the clarification process, they tend to draw out flavor. A variety of other ingredients — among them meat, aromatic vegetables, herbs and seasonings — are included for their flavor-giving properties.*

The consommé may be garnished with a variety of cut vegetables (overleaf). Typically, only one garnish is presented in each bowl; if the vegetables are cut into brunoise, however, they may be paired to provide intriguing contrasts of color. Root vegetables such as carrots, turnips and rutabagas should be blanched in boiling water for 30 seconds before being used as garnishes.

A Simple Way to Clarify Stock

1 *ADDING THE CLARIFICATION MIXTURE. Bring 2 quarts of stock to a boil (for illustrative purposes, a clear pot is used here). Pour in the freshly prepared clarification mixture (recipe above). Scrape the bowl, if necessary, to dislodge the last of the mixture.*

2 *STIRRING IN THE MIXTURE. With a long-handled wooden spoon, immediately stir the clarification mixture and the stock together to incorporate the clarification mixture into the liquid. Adjust the heat so that the stock simmers; it should not be allowed to boil vigorously.*

3 *FORMING THE RAFT. Within a few minutes, the clarification mixture will float to the surface in a layer, creating a kind of raft. Locate a hole or fissure in the raft and gently enlarge it just enough to allow the stock to bubble through. Simmer the stock for 30 minutes more before straining it.*

Edible Adornments for Consommé

A Garnish of Tomato Julienne

1 *REMOVING THE FLESH. Cut a shallow cross in the bottom of a tomato; blanch the tomato in boiling water for 15 seconds, then cool it immediately in cold water and peel off its skin. Place the tomato, stem end down, on a cutting board. Following the contour of the fruit, use a small knife to cut away the outer flesh in thin pieces (above).*

2 *CUTTING STRIPS. Lay a piece of tomato flat on the work surface and slice it lengthwise into strips about ⅛ inch wide (above). Repeat the process to julienne the other pieces; present the tomato julienne in the soup as pictured at right.*

Carrot Flowers

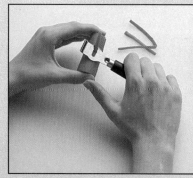

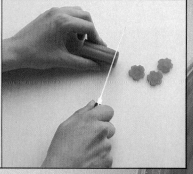

1 *SCORING THE CARROT. Cut a 2-inch segment from the stem end of a peeled carrot. Score a lengthwise groove in the segment by drawing a channel knife from one end to the other (above). Cut two or four additional evenly spaced channels in the segment. (Alternatively, notch an odd number of shallow grooves in the carrot segment with a paring knife.)*

2 *MAKING FLOWERS. Using a thin-bladed knife (here, a utility knife) shave thin rounds from the carrot segment to produce flowers. Blanch the flowers for 30 seconds before adding them to consommé.*

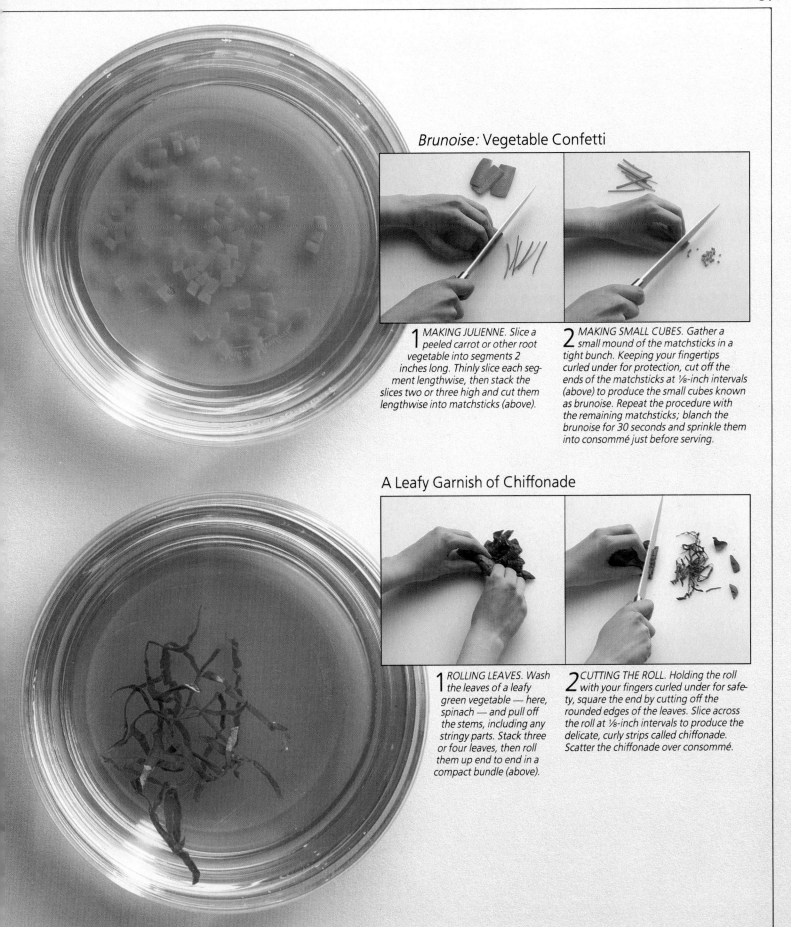

Brunoise: Vegetable Confetti

1 *MAKING JULIENNE. Slice a peeled carrot or other root vegetable into segments 2 inches long. Thinly slice each segment lengthwise, then stack the slices two or three high and cut them lengthwise into matchsticks (above).*

2 *MAKING SMALL CUBES. Gather a small mound of the matchsticks in a tight bunch. Keeping your fingertips curled under for protection, cut off the ends of the matchsticks at ⅛-inch intervals (above) to produce the small cubes known as brunoise. Repeat the procedure with the remaining matchsticks; blanch the brunoise for 30 seconds and sprinkle them into consommé just before serving.*

A Leafy Garnish of Chiffonade

1 *ROLLING LEAVES. Wash the leaves of a leafy green vegetable — here, spinach — and pull off the stems, including any stringy parts. Stack three or four leaves, then roll them up end to end in a compact bundle (above).*

2 *CUTTING THE ROLL. Holding the roll with your fingers curled under for safety, square the end by cutting off the rounded edges of the leaves. Slice across the roll at ⅛-inch intervals to produce the delicate, curly strips called chiffonade. Scatter the chiffonade over consommé.*

Beef and Capellini Soup with Scallions and Red Pepper

Serves 4
Working time: about 30 minutes
Total time: about 1 hour and 30 minutes
(includes marinating)

Calories **230**
Protein **23g.**
Cholesterol **39mg.**
Total fat **7g.**
Saturated fat **3g.**
Sodium **445mg.**

8 oz. beef tenderloin, trimmed of all visible fat and cut into thin strips about 1-inch long
1 tbsp. low-sodium soy sauce
1 tbsp. dry sherry
2 oz. capellini or other very thin pasta, broken into 1-inch lengths
8 cups unsalted brown stock
8 oz. celery cabbage, cut into ¼-inch-wide strips
1 sweet red pepper, sliced into very thin strips
8 oz. firm tofu (bean curd), cut into ½-inch cubes, each cube halved diagonally
4 garlic cloves, finely chopped
1 tbsp. white vinegar
3 scallions, trimmed, the green parts sliced diagonally into thin ovals, the white parts reserved for another use
freshly ground black pepper

Combine the beef strips, soy sauce and sherry in a bowl. Marinate the beef at room temperature for at least one hour.

Meanwhile, add the capellini to 4 cups of boiling water with ½ teaspoon of salt. Start testing the pasta after two minutes and cook it until it is *al dente*. Drain the pasta, rinse it under cold running water to keep it from sticking together, and set it aside.

Bring the stock to a boil in a large pot. Add the celery cabbage and cook it for five minutes. Stir in the red pepper and cook the mixture until the cabbage and red pepper are tender — about two minutes more. Add the tofu, the capellini, and the beef and its marinade. Reduce the heat and simmer the soup until the beef is cooked — about two minutes. Just before serving, stir in the garlic, vinegar, scallions and a generous grinding of pepper.

Chicken Soup with Carrots, Potatoes and Spinach

Serves 4
Working time: about 30 minutes
Total time: about 1 hour and 30 minutes

Calories **290**
Protein **27g.**
Cholesterol **71mg.**
Total fat **6g.**
Saturated fat **2g.**
Sodium **430mg.**

1 small chicken (about 2 lb.), skinned, all visible fat removed
1 onion, peeled and stuck with 2 cloves
1 celery stalk
8 to 12 parsley stems
1 bay leaf
1 tsp. ground cumin
1 sprig fresh thyme, or ¼ tsp. dried thyme leaves
1 whole bulb of garlic, outer papery coating removed, the bulb cut in half crosswise
½ tsp. salt
¾ lb. boiling potatoes, peeled and sliced (about 2 cups)
1 lb. carrots, sliced into ¼-inch-thick rounds
4 oz. fresh spinach, washed, stemmed and sliced into ½-inch-wide strips
freshly ground black pepper

Put the chicken into a large pot and add 6 cups of water. Bring the water to a boil, then reduce the heat and simmer the chicken for 10 minutes, frequently skimming off the foam that rises to the surface. Add the onion, celery, parsley stems, bay leaf, cumin, thyme, garlic and salt and continue simmering until the chicken is tender — about 45 minutes.

Place a colander over a large bowl and pour the contents of the pot into it. Leave the chicken to cool in the colander.

Return the broth to the pot and bring it to a boil. Add the potatoes, reduce the heat, and cover the pot; then simmer until the potatoes are just tender — about 10 minutes. Remove the potatoes with a slotted spoon and set them aside.

Add the carrots to the simmering broth, cover the pot, and continue to cook until the carrots are very tender — 15 to 20 minutes.

While the carrots are cooking, remove the meat from the chicken and either cut it or tear it with your fingers into bite-size pieces. Reserve the meat; discard the bones and the remaining solids in the colander.

When the carrots are cooked, purée half of them with half of the broth in a food processor or blender. Transfer the contents to a bowl; then purée the remaining carrots and broth. Pour all the liquid back into the pot. Add the potatoes, chicken and spinach leaves. Reheat the soup gently and season it with pepper.

Duck Soup with Endive and Caramelized Pears

Serves 6
Working time: about 1 hour
Total time: about 3 hours

Calories **225**
Protein **20g.**
Cholesterol **67mg.**
Total fat **11g.**
Saturated fat **5g.**
Sodium **60mg.**

one 4-lb. duck, skinned (page 55), the meat removed from the bones and carcass, trimmed of all fat and cut into ½-inch cubes, the carcass, bones and giblets reserved
1 tsp. Sichuan peppercorns, toasted and ground
1 onion, sliced
2 slices fresh ginger, each about ⅛ inch thick
1 small Belgian endive, sliced
1 tbsp. safflower oil
2 ripe but firm Bartlett pears, peeled, quartered, cored and cut into thick slices
2 tsp. sugar
2 tbsp. red wine vinegar
3 scallions, trimmed, the green parts sliced, the white parts reserved for another use

Toss the cubes of duck meat with the ground peppercorns and refrigerate them while you make the stock.

To prepare the stock, first chop the duck carcass into three or four pieces with a large, heavy knife, a cleaver or poultry shears. Put the pieces into a large, heavy-bottomed pot along with the other bones and the giblets. Set the pot over medium heat and cook the bones and giblets for about five minutes. Pour in enough water (about 8 cups) to cover the bones, then add the onion and the ginger. Bring the water to a boil, skimming any foam from the surface. Simmer the stock for at least two hours. Strain it into a large bowl and degrease it *(box, page 55)*.

While the stock is simmering, parboil the endive: Bring 4 cups of water to a boil in a saucepan over medium-high heat. Add the endive and cook it until it is tender — about five minutes. Drain the endive and set it aside.

Heat the oil in another large, heavy-bottomed pot over medium heat. Add the cubes of duck meat and cook them, stirring frequently, until they are browned on all sides — about five minutes. Remove the cubes with a slotted spoon and set them aside.

Add the pear slices to the pot and cook them until they are translucent but still firm — about 5 minutes. Sprinkle the sugar over the pears and continue cooking them, stirring gently but constantly, until the sugar melts. Pour in the vinegar and cook the slices for two minutes more. Remove the pear slices and set them aside with the duck.

Pour the duck stock into the pot and bring the liquid to a boil, scraping the bottom and sides of the pot to dissolve the caramelized juices. Add the endive slices, duck, caramelized pears and scallions to the soup; return it to a boil and serve it at once.

Degreasing Soups and Stews

A pivotal step in making soups and stews as healthful as they can be is degreasing — the removal of fat from the surface of the cooking liquid. The means for achieving this are varied, both in the time they consume and in the tools they require.

The easiest and most effective degreasing method is to refrigerate the finished dish, then lift the congealed layer of fat from the surface. Because chilling takes time, it is ideal for soups, stews or stocks that are made ahead. To inhibit bacterial growth, a hot soup or stew should be quickly cooled to room temperature, then partially covered and refrigerated. The fat may then be removed before the dish is reheated. Stock, too, should be cooled rapidly: Pour it into small containers and set them in a shallow bath of ice water. So that the stock will not sour, it should be covered and refrigerated only when it has cooled. Before transferring chilled stock to the freezer, scrape away all surface fat.

To degrease a hot dish just before serving it, use a soup ladle or a large, shallow spoon to skim off as much fat as you can; tip the pot, if need be, to pool the last bit of unwanted fat.

If you are making consommé, which must be served fat free, lightly draw an ice cube across the surface; the fat will cling to the cube. Alternatively, blot up any remaining fat with paper towels: Lay a corner or strip of towel directly on the fat, then immediately lift away the towel. Continue this process, always using a dry section of towel, to rid the surface of every drop of fat.

A hot liquid may also be defatted with a degreasing cup, a curious-looking clear pitcher whose spout rises from the bottom rather than the top. First strain the soup, stew or stock, then ladle the strained liquid into the degreasing cup and let it stand; the fat will rise to the surface. Tipping the cup at a slight angle, slowly pour the liquid from the spout; stop pouring when the layer of fat nears the spout opening at the bottom. Rinse the cup with hot water, then repeat the procedure to degrease the remaining liquid.

Skinning a Duck

1 *REMOVING THE WINGS. Pull out and discard the pockets of fat just inside the duck's tail cavity. Cut off and discard the tail and the flap of neck skin. With the duck breast side down, pull a wing away from the body and cut through the joint with a boning knife (below). Sever the other wing likewise; use the wings for stock.*

2 *SPLITTING THE SKIN. Cut through the skin along the backbone from one end of the bird to the other as demonstrated below. Turn the duck onto its back and make another straight cut from end to end to split the skin on the breast side.*

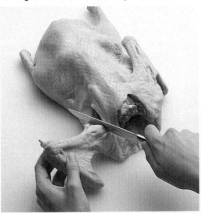

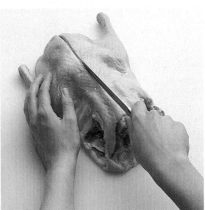

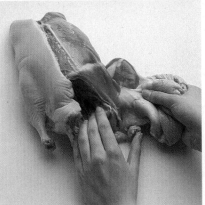

3 *SKINNING THE BODY. At one end of the cut on the breast side, pull away a small flap of skin; insert the knife tip between skin and flesh. Holding the skin taut, cut against it with short strokes to detach the skin, lifting it off with your free hand (above). Turn the bird onto its breast; starting at the neck end of the split, detach the skin on the same half of the duck from the neck to below the thigh joint.*

4 *SKINNING THE LEG. Turn the duck onto its back again and gather the detached skin in one hand. Steadying the bird with your other hand, pull the skin down over the leg as shown. (Where the skin adheres firmly to the meat, pull it taut and cut it away.) Trim off any skin still attached to the tail area. Repeat steps 3 and 4 to skin the duck's other side.*

ing ½ tablespoon of sage, the carrots, the remaining ¼ teaspoon of salt and some pepper. Bring the liquid to a simmer over medium heat and cook it for about 10 minutes.

While the stock is simmering, pour the oil into a nonstick or heavy-bottomed skillet over medium-high heat. Arrange the meatballs in the hot oil, taking care that they do not touch one another. Cook the meatballs on one side until they are well browned — three to five minutes. Continue to cook the meatballs, turning them frequently, until they are browned on all sides — five to seven minutes more.

With a slotted spoon, transfer the meatballs to the simmering stock mixture in the pot. Add the pasta and cook it until it is *al dente* — about four minutes.

Transfer the soup to individual serving bowls; garnish with the sage leaves if you are using them, and serve immediately.

Veal and Noodle Soup with Sage

Serves 6
Working time: about 40 minutes
Total time: about 1 hour and 10 minutes

Calories **240**
Protein **17g.**
Cholesterol **75mg.**
Total fat **7g.**
Saturated fat **2g.**
Sodium **385mg.**

12 oz. lean veal, finely chopped, or 12 oz. ground veal
1 egg, beaten with 1 egg white
1½ tbsp. chopped fresh sage, or 2 tsp. dried sage
2 tbsp. freshly grated Parmesan or Romano cheese
2 slices day-old white bread, crumbled
1 plum tomato, seeded and finely chopped
½ cup very finely chopped onion
5 garlic cloves, finely chopped
½ tsp. salt
freshly ground black pepper
4 cups unsalted veal stock
2 carrots, thinly sliced
1 tbsp. safflower oil
4 oz. angel-hair pasta (capellini)
fresh sage leaves for garnish (optional)

In a large bowl, combine the veal, egg mixture, 1 tablespoon of the sage, the cheese, bread, tomato, onion, garlic, ¼ teaspoon of the salt and some pepper. Cover the bowl with plastic wrap and refrigerate it for 30 minutes. Form the chilled mixture into 18 meatballs, each about 1 inch in diameter. Set the meatballs aside.

Pour the stock into a large pot. Add the remain-

Sake-Simmered Velvet Chicken Soup

THE "VELVET" IN THE TITLE REFERS TO THE SMOOTH COATING OF CORNSTARCH THAT ENVELOPS THE CHICKEN, SEALING IN ITS SUCCULENT JUICES.

Serves 2
Working time: about 30 minutes
Total time: about 45 minutes

Calories **340**
Protein **30g.**
Cholesterol **69mg.**
Total fat **6g.**
Saturated fat **2g.**
Sodium **320mg.**

8 oz. boneless chicken breast or thigh meat, skinned, trimmed of all fat and cut into ½-inch cubes
1 tbsp. cornstarch
2½ cups unsalted chicken stock
¼ cup sake or rice wine
1 tsp. low-sodium soy sauce
1 to 2 tbsp. finely chopped fresh ginger
2 carrots, sliced into ½-inch-thick rounds
2 or 3 parsnips, peeled and sliced into ½-inch-thick rounds
4 scallions, trimmed and sliced diagonally into thin ovals

Pour 4 cups of water into a saucepan and bring it to a boil. Toss the chicken cubes with the cornstarch to coat them evenly, then add them to the boiling water; stir with a slotted spoon to separate the cubes. When the water returns to a boil, remove the chicken pieces and set them aside. Discard the water.

Add the stock to the saucepan along with the sake or rice wine, the soy sauce and the ginger. Bring the liquid to a boil, then add the chicken cubes, carrots and parsnips. Reduce the heat to low, cover the pan, and simmer the soup for 15 minutes. Stir the scallions into the soup two minutes before serving.

Lamb and Wild-Rice Soup

Serves 6
Working time: about 50 minutes
Total time: about 2 hours

Calories **375**
Protein **19g.**
Cholesterol **1mg.**
Total fat **13g.**
Saturated fat **6g.**
Sodium **275mg.**

1 tbsp. safflower oil
2 lamb shanks (about 2 lb.), trimmed of fat
3 large onions (about 1½ lb.), coarsely chopped
2 cups dry white wine
14 oz. canned unsalted tomatoes, drained and chopped
3 cups unsalted chicken or veal stock
1 carrot, sliced into ¼-inch-thick rounds
8 garlic cloves, chopped
1 celery stalk, chopped
freshly ground black pepper
½ tsp. salt
1½ tbsp. fresh rosemary, or 1 tsp. dried rosemary
1 cup wild rice

Heat the oil in a large, heavy-bottomed skillet over medium-high heat. Sauté the lamb shanks in the skillet until they are dark brown all over — about 15 minutes. Transfer the browned lamb shanks to a large pot.

Reduce the heat under the skillet to medium. Add the onions and cook them, stirring frequently, until they are lightly browned — 10 to 15 minutes.

Add the browned onions to the pot with the lamb shanks. Return the skillet to the heat and immediately pour in the wine. With a wooden spoon, scrape up the caramelized pan juices from the bottom of the skillet, stirring well to dissolve them. Add the tomatoes and boil the mixture until it is reduced by half — about five minutes. Pour the reduced liquid over the lamb and onions in the pot, then add the stock, 10 cups of water, the carrot, garlic, celery and some pepper.

Place the pot over medium heat and bring the mixture to a strong simmer, skimming off any foam that rises to the surface. Stir in the salt and rosemary. Reduce the heat and gently simmer the soup until the lamb is tender — one and one half to two hours.

After the meat has cooked for one hour, put the rice

into a saucepan with 1 cup of water and bring the liquid to a simmer over medium heat. Reduce the heat to low and cook the rice slowly until all of the water is absorbed — about 15 minutes. Set the rice aside.

Transfer the lamb shanks to a clean work surface.

When they are cool enough to handle, remove the meat from the bones. Cut the meat into small pieces; discard the bones. Return the meat to the pot. Add the partially cooked rice and simmer the soup until the rice is tender — about 20 minutes. Serve the soup hot.

Chicken, Eggplant and Tomato Soup

Serves 4
Working (and total) time: about 1 hour

Calories **280**
Protein **27g.**
Cholesterol **63mg.**
Total fat **9g.**
Saturated fat **4g.**
Sodium **380mg.**

8 cups unsalted chicken stock
4 garlic cloves, finely chopped
juice of 1 lemon
freshly ground black pepper
4 chicken breast halves, skinned and boned (about 1 lb.)
1 tbsp. chopped fresh mint
2½ lb. ripe tomatoes, peeled, seeded and coarsely chopped, or 28 oz. canned unsalted tomatoes, drained and chopped
1 tbsp. fresh thyme, or ¾ tsp. dried thyme leaves
¾ lb. unpeeled eggplant, cut into ½-inch cubes
2 oz. feta cheese, soaked 10 minutes in cold water to remove some of its salt, drained and crumbled

Bring the stock to a boil in a large, heavy-bottomed saucepan. Add the garlic, half of the lemon juice and a generous grinding of pepper; reduce the heat and add the chicken. Poach the chicken at a simmer until the meat feels springy to the touch — about five minutes.

Use a slotted spoon to remove the chicken from the poaching liquid. When the chicken is cool enough to handle, cut it into small cubes and put the cubes in a bowl. Toss the chicken with the mint and the remaining lemon juice, and set it aside to marinate.

Add the tomatoes and thyme to the stock, and simmer the liquid for 10 minutes. Add the eggplant and cook for five minutes more. Stir in the chicken and its marinade and simmer the soup for two minutes. Serve the soup with the cheese sprinkled on top.

Chicken Soup with Chilies, Cabbage and Rice

Serves 4
Working time: about 20 minutes
Total time: about 1 hour

Calories **285**
Protein **20g.**
Cholesterol **58mg.**
Total fat **11g.**
Saturated fat **2g.**
Sodium **275mg.**

1 tbsp. safflower oil
1½ lb. chicken thighs, skinned, fat trimmed away
1 garlic clove, finely chopped
3 scallions, trimmed and sliced into thin rounds
2 cups unsalted chicken stock
1 tbsp. fresh thyme, or ¾ tsp. dried thyme leaves
freshly ground black pepper
¼ tsp. salt
½ cup rice
2 dried ancho chilies, stemmed, split lengthwise and seeded
1 large carrot, julienned (about 1 cup)
2 cups shredded Nappa cabbage (about 6 oz.)

Heat the safflower oil in a large, heavy-bottomed pot over medium-high heat. Add the chicken thighs and sauté them, turning them frequently, until they are evenly browned — three to four minutes. Push the chicken to one side of the pot; add the garlic and scallions and cook them for one minute, stirring con-

stantly. Pour in the stock and 3 cups of water. Add the thyme and some pepper, and bring the liquid to a boil. Reduce the heat to maintain a simmer and cook the mixture, partially covered, for 20 minutes. Skim any impurities from the surface and simmer the liquid for 20 minutes more.

While the stock is simmering, bring 1 cup of water and ⅛ teaspoon of the salt to a boil in a saucepan. Add the rice and stir once, then reduce the heat and cover the pan. Simmer the rice until all of the water is absorbed — about 20 minutes.

While the rice is cooking, pour 1 cup of boiling water over the chilies and soak them for 15 minutes. Purée the chilies with their soaking liquid in a blender. (Alternatively, pulverize the soaked chilies with a mortar and pestle, gradually adding the soaking liquid until it is incorporated into the chili paste.)

With a slotted spoon, remove the chicken thighs from the pot and set them aside. When the chicken is cool enough to handle, remove the meat from the bones with your fingers and cut it into small pieces; discard the bones. Return the chicken pieces to the pot. Add the carrot, cabbage, rice and the remaining ⅛ teaspoon of salt. Increase the heat to maintain a simmer and cook the soup until the carrot is tender — three to four minutes. Strain the chili purée through a fine sieve into the soup. Stir to incorporate the purée and serve the soup at once.

Beef Soup with Brussels Sprouts and Sweet Potato

Serves 4
Working time: about 30 minutes
Total time: about 1 hour and 30 minutes

Calories **225**
Protein **28g.**
Cholesterol **77mg.**
Total fat **7g.**
Saturated fat **3g.**
Sodium **190mg.**

1 lb. beef-shank bones
1 lb. lean beef, finely diced
1 small onion, thinly sliced
1 garlic clove, finely chopped
1 small bay leaf
4 oz. fresh Brussels sprouts, trimmed and halved lengthwise
1 sweet potato (about 5 oz.), peeled and cut into ¾-inch cubes
1 tsp. finely chopped fresh rosemary, or ½ tsp. dried rosemary
¼ tsp. salt
freshly ground black pepper

Place the shank bones, beef, onion, garlic and bay leaf in a large, heavy-bottomed pot. Pour in 10 cups of water and bring it to a boil. Reduce the heat to maintain a strong simmer. Cook the mixture, partially covered, for one hour, occasionally skimming off the impurities that rise to the surface.

Remove and discard the bones and bay leaf. Increase the heat to high and cook the mixture until the liquid is reduced to about 3 cups — 10 to 15 minutes. Add the Brussels sprouts, sweet potato and rosemary. Reduce the heat and simmer the soup until the vegetables are tender — eight to 10 minutes. Stir in the salt and some pepper, and serve the soup immediately.

Pork Soup with Nappa Cabbage

Serves 6
Working (and total) time: about 25 minutes

Calories **230**
Protein **20g.**
Cholesterol **49mg.**
Total fat **5g.**
Saturated fat **1g.**
Sodium **300mg.**

¼ cup rice wine or dry sherry
2 tbsp. cornstarch
1 tbsp. finely chopped fresh ginger
1 lb. pork tenderloin, trimmed of all fat and thinly sliced across the grain
4 oz. vermicelli or thin egg noodles
¼ tsp. salt
6 dried Asian mushrooms, covered with boiling water and soaked for 20 minutes, stemmed and thinly sliced, the soaking liquid reserved
6 cups unsalted chicken stock
3 tbsp. rice vinegar
2 tsp. bean paste
8 oz. Nappa cabbage, thinly sliced
⅓ cup cilantro leaves
½ tsp. dark sesame oil

Pour the wine into a nonreactive bowl and stir in the cornstarch and ginger. Add the pork and stir gently to coat it with the liquid. Set the bowl aside.

Add the vermicelli or noodles to 4 cups of boiling water with ¼ teaspoon of salt. Start testing the pasta after three minutes and cook it until it is *al dente*. Drain and rinse it under cold running water and set it aside.

Carefully pour ½ cup of the mushroom-soaking liquid into a measuring cup, leaving the grit behind, then pour the ½ cup of liquid into a large, heavy-bottomed pot. Add the mushrooms, stock, vinegar and bean paste. Bring the liquid to a boil, then stir in the pork slices along with their marinade and the cabbage. Return the liquid to a boil and add the vermicelli or noodles, cilantro and sesame oil. Cook the soup until the pasta is heated through — about two minutes. Transfer the soup to a warmed bowl and serve it at once.

Turkey-Lentil Soup

Serves 6
Working time: about 15 minutes
Total time: about 1 hour

Calories **220**
Protein **22g.**
Cholesterol **44mg.**
Total fat **5g.**
Saturated fat **1g.**
Sodium **185mg.**

1 ½ lb. turkey drumsticks, skinned
freshly ground black pepper
2 tsp. safflower oil
1 small onion, thinly sliced
1 cup lentils, picked over and rinsed
1 small bay leaf
1 small carrot, thinly sliced
1 small zucchini, thinly sliced
1 celery stalk, thinly sliced
1 ripe tomato, peeled, seeded and coarsely chopped
½ tsp. finely chopped fresh sage, or ¼ tsp. dried sage
⅜ tsp. salt

Sprinkle the drumsticks with some pepper. Heat the oil in a large, heavy-bottomed pot over medium heat. Add the drumsticks and cook them, turning them fre-quently, until they are evenly browned — two to three minutes. Push the drumsticks to one side of the pan, then add the onion and cook it until it is translucent — two to three minutes.

Pour 5 cups of water into the pot. Add the lentils and bay leaf, and bring the water to a boil. Reduce the heat to maintain a simmer and cook the lentils, covered, for 20 minutes. Skim off any impurities that have risen to the surface. Continue cooking the mixture until the juices run clear from a drumstick pierced with the tip of a sharp knife — about 20 minutes more.

Remove the drumsticks and set them aside. When they are cool enough to handle, slice the meat from the bones and cut it into small pieces; discard the bones. Remove and discard the bay leaf. Add the car-rot, zucchini, celery and tomato to the soup and sim-mer until the vegetables are tender — about five min-utes. Add the turkey meat, sage and salt, and continue cooking the soup until the vegetables are tender — about two minutes more. Serve hot.

Lamb Broth
with Winter Vegetables

Serves 6
Working time: about 15 minutes
Total time: about 2 hours

Calories **205**
Protein **9g.**
Cholesterol **33mg.**
Total fat **14g.**
Saturated fat **7g.**
Sodium **225mg.**

1 tbsp. safflower oil
1 small onion, thinly sliced, the slices separated into rings
1½ lb. lamb shank, trimmed
¼ cup pearl barley
1 bay leaf
1 tsp. chopped fresh thyme, or ¼ tsp. dried thyme leaves
1 garlic clove, finely chopped
½ tsp. salt
¼ tsp. crushed black peppercorns
1 turnip, peeled and cut into ½-inch cubes
1 small rutabaga, peeled and cut into ½-inch cubes
1 carrot, cut into ½-inch cubes

Heat the oil in a large, heavy-bottomed pot over medium heat. Add the onion rings and cook them until they are browned — about eight minutes. Add the lamb shank, barley, bay leaf, thyme, garlic, salt and crushed peppercorns. Pour in 12 cups of water and bring the liquid to a boil. Reduce the heat and simmer the mixture, partially covered, for one hour and 15 minutes.

Remove the bay leaf and discard it. Remove the lamb shank from the pot; when the shank is cool enough to handle, slice the meat from the bone and cut it into small cubes. Return the lamb cubes to the pot. Simmer the soup, uncovered, over medium heat until it is reduced by half — about 15 minutes. Add the turnip, rutabaga and carrot, cover the pot, and simmer the soup until the vegetables are tender — about 15 minutes more. Serve immediately.

Vegetable Soup with Grilled Chicken

Serves 4
Working time: about 30 minutes
Total time: about 1 hour

Calories **255**
Protein **16g.**
Cholesterol **26mg.**
Total fat **10g.**
Saturated fat **2g.**
Sodium **320mg.**

2 chicken breast halves, skinned and boned (about 8 oz.)	¼ tsp. ground cumin
1 tsp. olive oil	½ tsp. dried oregano
juice of 1 lime	¼ tsp. salt
freshly ground black pepper	1 carrot, julienned
1 large red onion, chopped	1 zucchini, julienned
2 garlic cloves, finely chopped	4 oz. jícama, julienned
6 cups unsalted chicken stock	1 tbsp. finely cut chives
1 lb. ripe plum tomatoes, peeled, seeded and chopped, or 14 oz. canned unsalted tomatoes, drained and chopped	**Tortilla-strip garnish**
⅛ tsp. ground coriander	3 corn tortillas
⅛ tsp. cayenne pepper	1 tbsp. olive oil

Using a boning knife or other thin-bladed knife, cut each chicken breast half horizontally into two thin, flat pieces. Set the pieces on a large plate, drizzle the teaspoon of oil and the lime juice over them and sprinkle them with some pepper. Let the chicken marinate while you make the rest of the soup.

Combine the onion, garlic and stock in a saucepan over medium-high heat. Bring the stock to a boil, then add the tomatoes, coriander, cayenne pepper, cumin, oregano and salt. Reduce the heat and simmer the mixture for 20 minutes. Add the carrot, zucchini and jícama, and simmer them until they are tender — about six minutes.

Just before the vegetables are done, prepare the chicken and the garnish. Preheat the grill or broiler.

Remove the chicken from the marinade and cook it until it is firm to the touch — about two minutes on each side. Cut the pieces on the diagonal into thin slices.

Brush the tortillas with the tablespoon of olive oil and cut them into thin strips. Spread the strips out on a baking sheet and broil them until they are crisp and lightly browned — about three minutes.

Arrange the chicken slices on top of the soup and sprinkle it with the chives. Serve the tortilla strips in a bowl alongside.

Turkey Goulash Soup

Serves 6
Working time: about 30 minutes
Total time: about 45 minutes

Calories **260**
Protein **24g.**
Cholesterol **41mg.**
Total fat **6g.**
Saturated fat **1g.**
Sodium **290mg.**

2 tsp. safflower oil
3 onions (about 1 lb.), thinly sliced
2 green peppers, seeded, deribbed and cut into ¾-inch squares
2 tbsp. paprika, preferably Hungarian
¼ tsp. ground cumin
freshly ground black pepper
8 cups unsalted chicken stock
2 tbsp. cornstarch
4 oz. wide egg noodles
1 lb. turkey cutlets, sliced across the grain into 2-inch-long strips
⅜ tsp. salt

Heat the safflower oil in a large, heavy-bottomed pot over medium heat. Add the sliced onions and cook them until they are browned — about 15 minutes. Stir in the green peppers, paprika, cumin, some black pepper and all except ¼ cup of the stock. Combine the cornstarch and the reserved stock, and add this mixture to the pot. Simmer the stock, partially covered, for 20 minutes.

While the stock is simmering, add the noodles to 8 cups of boiling water with ½ teaspoon of salt. Start testing the noodles after five minutes and cook them until they are *al dente*. Drain the noodles, rinse them under cold running water, and set them aside.

Add the turkey strips to the simmering stock and poach them until they are opaque — three to four minutes. Stir in the noodles and the ⅜ teaspoon of salt. Cook the soup for two minutes more; serve at once.

Turkey Soup with Lemon-Celery Dumplings

Serves 6
Working time: about 45 minutes
Total time: about 2 hours and 20 minutes

Calories **320**
Protein **33g.**
Cholesterol **72mg.**
Total fat **8g.**
Saturated fat **3g.**
Sodium **515mg.**

4 turkey-wing drumettes (about 2 lb.)
2 carrots, sliced into thin rounds
2 onions, coarsely chopped
¾ tsp. ground allspice
2 celery stalks, thinly sliced
2 tbsp. fresh lemon juice
5 garlic cloves, finely chopped
½ tsp. salt
freshly ground black pepper

Lemon-celery dumplings
1⅓ cups unbleached all-purpose flour
2 tsp. double-acting baking powder
¼ tsp. salt
⅛ tsp. cayenne pepper
3 tbsp. finely chopped celery leaves
1 tbsp. safflower oil
1 tbsp. unsalted butter, melted
½ cup low-fat milk
1 tbsp. fresh lemon juice
1 tsp. grated lemon zest

Place the turkey-wing drumettes in a large, heavy-bottomed pot. Pour in 12 cups of water and bring it to a boil. Reduce the heat to medium and cook the drumettes for five minutes, skimming off any impurities that collect on the surface of the liquid. Pour in ½ cup of cold water, and simmer the turkey for 20 minutes,

skimming as necessary. Add the carrots, onions, all-spice, celery, lemon juice, garlic, salt and some pepper. Simmer the mixture until the turkey is quite tender — about one and a half hours.

About half an hour before the turkey is done, prepare the dumpling dough: Sift the flour, baking powder, salt and cayenne pepper into a large bowl. Stir in the celery leaves, oil and butter to obtain a dry paste. Whisk in the milk ¼ cup at a time, then whisk in the lemon juice and lemon zest until the dough becomes smooth and elastic. Cover the bowl with plastic wrap and refrigerate it.

When the turkey is tender, strain the liquid into a large bowl. Remove the wings from the strainer and set them aside. Degrease the liquid (box, page 55). Purée the vegetables with a little of the cooking liquid in a blender or food processor. Return the purée and

the degreased liquid to the pot.

When the turkey drumettes are cool enough to handle, peel off and discard their skin. Remove the meat from the bones; discard the bones. Cut the meat into ½-inch pieces and return it to the soup.

Bring the soup to a simmer. Spoon heaping teaspoons of the dough directly into the soup, rinsing the spoon in cold water after each dumpling floats free. Simmer the dumplings on the first side for five minutes, then gently turn them over and simmer them on the second side until they are lightly puffed up — three to five minutes more. Serve the soup and dumplings immediately.

EDITOR'S NOTE: Turkey-wing "drumettes" — the upper parts of the wings, which contain most of the meat — are widely available in supermarkets.

Beef and Wild Mushroom Soup

Serves 8
Working time: about 50 minutes
Total time: about 1 hour

Calories **185**
Protein **17g.**
Cholesterol **41mg.**
Total fat **8g.**
Saturated fat **2g.**
Sodium **375mg.**

10 dried shiitake or Asian black mushrooms, covered with 2 cups of boiling water and soaked for 20 minutes
6 cups unsalted chicken stock
2 tbsp. safflower oil
1 lb. top sirloin, trimmed of fat and cut into ½-inch-wide strips
5 garlic cloves, finely chopped
2 onions, finely chopped (about 1½ cups)
4 oz. fresh shiitake mushrooms, stems trimmed, thinly sliced
8 oz. button mushrooms, stems trimmed, thinly sliced
½ tsp. salt
½ cup Madeira, dry sherry or Marsala
freshly ground black pepper
2 tbsp. low-sodium soy sauce
2 tbsp. chopped fresh parsley, preferably Italian

Remove the soaked mushrooms from their liquid; reserve the liquid. Cut off and discard the stems. Thinly slice the caps and set them aside. Slowly pour all but about ½ cup of the mushroom-soaking liquid into a large pot, leaving the grit behind; discard the gritty liquid. Add the chicken stock to the pot and bring the liquid to a simmer.

While the liquid is heating, pour 1 tablespoon of the oil into a large, heavy-bottomed skillet over medium-high heat. When the oil is hot, add the sirloin and sauté it, stirring constantly, for two minutes. Remove the beef and set it aside.

Pour the remaining tablespoon of oil into the skillet. Add the chopped garlic and onion and sauté them for 30 seconds, stirring constantly. Stir in all of the soaked and fresh mushrooms and ¼ teaspoon of the salt. Sauté the mixture, stirring frequently, for five minutes.

Pour in the Madeira, sherry or Marsala and stir to scrape up and dissolve any caramelized bits. Add the contents of the skillet to the simmering stock along with the remaining ¼ teaspoon of salt, some pepper and the soy sauce. Simmer the soup for 20 minutes.

Stir in the sautéed beef strips and cook for one minute more. Garnish the soup with the chopped parsley before serving.

Couscous Soup
with Harissa

HARISSA IS A HOT, SPICY MIXTURE USED TO FLAVOR NORTH
AFRICAN DISHES; IN THIS RECIPE, SOME PIMIENTOS ARE ADDED.

Serves 8
Working time: about 40 minutes
Total time: about 1 hour and 15 minutes

Calories **360**
Protein **25g.**
Cholesterol **51mg.**
Total fat **15g.**
Saturated fat **4g.**
Sodium **750mg.**

1 tbsp. olive oil
1 tbsp. unsalted butter
1 large onion, coarsely chopped (about 1½ cups)
½ tsp. cayenne pepper
½ tsp. ground cumin
½ tsp. cumin seeds
1 tsp. salt
½ tsp. cracked black peppercorns
½ tsp. ground allspice
4 tsp. chopped fresh thyme, or 1 tsp. dried thyme leaves
2 tsp. chopped fresh oregano, or ½ tsp. dried oregano
2 bay leaves
2 or 3 garlic cloves, finely chopped (about 1 tbsp.)
2½ lb. ripe tomatoes, peeled, seeded and chopped, or 28 oz. canned unsalted tomatoes, drained and chopped
8 cups unsalted chicken stock
1 large boiling potato, peeled and cut into ½-inch cubes
5 celery stalks, cut into ½-inch lengths (about 1½ cups)
3 carrots, sliced into ¼-inch-thick rounds (about 1½ cups)
1 lb. boneless chicken breast meat, cut into 1-inch cubes
4 oz. chorizo or other spicy sausage, cut into ½-inch-thick rounds
2 cups cooked and drained chick-peas
1 yellow squash and 1 zucchini, each cut lengthwise into 8 strips, the strips cut into 1-inch pieces (about 3 cups)
½ green pepper, seeded, deribbed and cut lengthwise into ¼-inch strips
½ sweet red pepper, seeded, deribbed and cut lengthwise into ¼-inch strips
¼ cup couscous

Harissa

6-oz. jar pimientos, drained
1 garlic clove
1 tsp. hot red-pepper sauce
2 tsp. chili paste
2 tsp. ground cumin
¼ tsp. salt

Heat the oil and butter together in a large, heavy-bottomed pot over medium-high heat. Add the onion and sauté it, stirring frequently, until it is translucent — about eight minutes.

Meanwhile, combine the spices with the thyme, oregano and bay leaves in a small bowl.

Add the garlic to the onions and cook the mixture, stirring constantly, for two minutes more. Add the combined spices and herbs, tomatoes and stock, then increase the heat, and bring the liquid to a boil. Stir in the potato, celery and carrots. Reduce the heat, cover the pot, and simmer the mixture until the potato cubes are tender — about 20 minutes.

Add the chicken, sausage, chick-peas, squash, peppers and couscous, and continue to simmer the soup for 20 minutes more.

While the soup finishes cooking, purée the harissa ingredients in a food processor or blender. Transfer the mixture to a small bowl to be passed at the table.

Serve the soup hot; allow each diner to add a dab of harissa if desired.

Crab, Fennel and Tomato Soup

Serves 4
Working time: about 45 minutes
Total time: about 2 hours

Calories **245**
Protein **9g.**
Cholesterol **31mg.**
Total fat **8g.**
Saturated fat **1g.**
Sodium **420mg.**

2 lb. live blue crabs (4 to 8 crabs)
2 tbsp. virgin olive oil
1 onion, thinly sliced
1 small fennel bulb, trimmed, cored and thinly sliced (about 2 cups), several stems and leaves reserved for the court bouillon and for garnish
3 garlic cloves, finely chopped
1 lb. ripe plum tomatoes, peeled, seeded and chopped, or 14 oz. canned unsalted tomatoes, drained and chopped
½ tsp. salt
cayenne pepper
Court bouillon
1 large onion, thinly sliced
1 celery stalk, thinly sliced
several parsley stems (optional)
2 cups dry white wine
8 to 10 peppercorns

To make the court bouillon, pour 8 cups of water into a large pot and add the onion, celery, reserved fennel stems and a few of the reserved fennel leaves, and the parsley stems if you are using them. Bring the liquid to a boil, then reduce the heat and simmer it for 15 minutes, skimming off any foam as it rises to the surface. Pour in the wine and return the liquid to a boil. Simmer the liquid for 10 minutes; add the peppercorns and simmer five minutes more.

Bring the court bouillon to a full boil and drop the crabs into it. Cover the pot until the liquid returns to a boil. Skim off any foam that rises to the surface, then reduce the heat and simmer the crabs, covered, for 20 minutes.

Strain the cooking liquid into a bowl. Set the crabs aside and discard the remaining solids. Return the cooking liquid to the pot and boil it until it is reduced to about 4 cups.

Heat the oil in another large pot over medium-low heat. Add the onion, fennel and garlic. Cover the pot and cook the vegetables, stirring occasionally, until they are soft — 10 to 15 minutes. Stir in the tomatoes, salt and a pinch of cayenne pepper. Pour in the reduced cooking liquid and bring the mixture to a boil. Reduce the heat and simmer the mixture, covered, until the fennel is very soft — about 45 minutes.

Remove the flesh from the crabs (there should be about 1 cup) and set it aside.

Purée the fennel-tomato mixture in batches in a blender or food processor until it is very smooth. Return the purée to the pot and add the crab meat. Cook the soup over medium-low heat until it is warmed through; garnish it with the remaining fennel leaves.

Key West Conch Chowder

FRESH OR FROZEN CONCH IS AVAILABLE WHOLE, POUNDED
INTO THIN STEAKS OR CHOPPED.

Serves 6
Working time: about 30 minutes
Total time: about 2 hours and 30 minutes

Calories **175**
Protein **10g.**
Cholesterol **109mg.**
Total fat **4g.**
Saturated fat **1g.**
Sodium **290mg.**

2 bacon strips, sliced into small pieces
2 onions, chopped
3 celery stalks, chopped
2 garlic cloves, finely chopped
1 lb. conch meat, finely chopped
42 oz. canned unsalted whole tomatoes, coarsely chopped, with their juice
2 cups fish stock or water
1 green pepper, seeded, deribbed and finely chopped
1 sweet red pepper, seeded, deribbed and finely chopped
1 ½ tsp. dried thyme leaves
1 ½ tsp. dried oregano
½ tsp. salt
1 tsp. freshly ground black pepper
1 bay leaf
2 large boiling potatoes, peeled and cut into ½-inch cubes (about 3 cups)
¼ cup dry sherry (optional)

Cook the bacon pieces in a large, heavy-bottomed pot over medium heat, stirring occasionally, until they are brown — about five minutes. Remove the bacon bits with a slotted spoon and set them aside on paper towels to drain. Pour out all but 2 tablespoons of the bacon fat and return the pot to the heat. Add the onions, celery and garlic; cook them, stirring frequently, until the onions are translucent — about 10 minutes.

Add the conch, tomatoes and their juice, stock or water, green and red peppers, thyme, oregano, salt, pepper and bay leaf to the pot. Bring the liquid to a boil, then reduce the heat and simmer the chowder, covered, until the conch is tender — about two hours. Stir the mixture from time to time to prevent sticking. If the chowder seems too thick at any point, pour in another cup of stock or water.

Add the potatoes and simmer them until they are tender — about 15 minutes. To serve the chowder, divide it among six bowls and garnish each portion with a few bacon bits. Add the sherry to taste — about 1 tablespoon per person — at the table.

EDITOR'S NOTE: *Quahog meat can be substituted for the conch, in which case the cooking time should be reduced to about one hour.*

Striped Bass and Sweet Pepper Soup

Serves 4
Working time: about 25 minutes
Total time: about 1 hour

Calories **125**
Protein **20g.**
Cholesterol **91mg.**
Total fat **3g.**
Saturated fat **1g.**
Sodium **135mg.**

1 lb. striped-bass or red-snapper fillets, the skin left on, rinsed, patted dry and cut into 1-inch cubes
2 tbsp. finely chopped fresh ginger
2 tbsp. dry sherry
6 cups fish stock
4 garlic cloves, thinly sliced
¼ tsp. salt
⅛ tsp. cayenne pepper
1 sweet red pepper, seeded, deribbed and cut into narrow strips about 1 inch long
1 yellow pepper, seeded, deribbed and cut into narrow strips about 1 inch long

Place the fish cubes in a shallow dish. Scatter the shredded ginger over them and pour in the sherry. Marinate the fish at room temperature for 30 minutes.

Meanwhile, pour the fish stock into a large, shallow pot and bring it to a boil. Stir in the sliced garlic, salt and cayenne pepper, and reduce the heat to maintain a strong simmer. Cook the mixture with the cover ajar for 30 minutes.

Add the pepper strips to the pot and cook them for three minutes. Pour the marinade into the pot and reduce the heat to maintain a gentle simmer. Add the fish and cook it gently until it is opaque and feels firm to the touch — about three minutes. Serve the hot soup immediately.

Blanch the julienned carrot in 2 cups of boiling water for two to three minutes. Remove the julienne with a slotted spoon and stir them into the soup.

Put the oysters and their liquid in a small saucepan over medium heat. Gently simmer the oysters until they begin to curl at the edges — three to four minutes. Transfer the oysters and their liquid to the soup; bring the soup to a simmer (do not let it boil) and add the watercress. Simmer the soup until the watercress is wilted — two to three minutes. Sprinkle the chives and paprika over the top, if you are using them, and serve the soup immediately.

Oyster Soup with Watercress and Carrot

Serves 4
Working time: about 40 minutes
Total time: about 1 hour

Calories **245**
Protein **14g.**
Cholesterol **72mg.**
Total fat **8g.**
Saturated fat **2g.**
Sodium **365mg.**

1 tbsp. safflower oil
1 onion, finely chopped
¼ lb. celeriac, peeled and finely chopped
1 potato, peeled and finely chopped
½ cup dry white wine
1½ cups fish stock
1 cup low-fat milk
cayenne pepper
¼ tsp. white pepper
¼ tsp. salt
1 large carrot, julienned
1 pint shucked oysters, the liquid reserved
2 cups watercress leaves
2 tsp. finely cut chives (optional)
1 tsp. paprika, preferably Hungarian (optional)

Heat the oil in a large, heavy-bottomed pot over medium-high heat. Add the onion and celeriac and cook them until the onion is translucent — four to five minutes. Add the potato, wine and stock, then reduce the heat and simmer the mixture, covered, until the vegetables are quite soft — 15 to 20 minutes. Purée the mixture in a blender or food processor and return it to the pot. Stir in the milk along with a pinch of cayenne pepper, the white pepper and salt.

Calories **140**
Protein **7g.**
Cholesterol **23mg.**
Total fat **4g.**
Saturated fat **1g.**
Sodium **40mg.**

Clam and Rice Soup

Serves 4
Working time: about 35 minutes
Total time: about 50 minutes

2 dozen littleneck clams, scrubbed
1 tbsp. virgin olive oil
½ cup finely chopped onion
2 tsp. finely chopped garlic
1 small bay leaf
¼ cup long-grain rice
¼ cup dry white wine
⅛ tsp. crushed saffron threads
½ tsp. fresh lemon juice
1 large, ripe tomato, peeled, seeded and finely chopped
2 tbsp. finely chopped fresh parsley

Bring 4 cups of water to a boil in a large pot. Add the clams, cover the pot tightly, and cook the clams until they open — about five minutes. Transfer the clams to a plate, discarding any that remain closed, and reserve the cooking liquid. When the clams are cool enough to handle, remove them from their shells. Discard the shells and set the clams aside.

Heat the oil in a heavy-bottomed skillet over medium heat. Add the onion, garlic and bay leaf, and sauté them, stirring frequently, until the onion is translucent — about five minutes.

Strain the clam-cooking liquid through a sieve lined with cheesecloth, then pour the liquid back into the pot. Add the contents of the skillet along with the rice, wine, saffron and lemon juice, and bring the mixture to a boil. Reduce the heat and cover the pot, leaving the lid ajar; simmer the mixture for 10 minutes, stirring once or twice. Add the tomato and simmer for five minutes more. Stir in the parsley and cook the soup for two minutes longer. Return the clams to the pot and heat them through. Serve the soup immediately.

Spinach and Fish Soup

Serves 6
Working time: about 25 minutes
Total time: about 1 hour

Calories **125**
Protein **17g.**
Cholesterol **7mg.**
Total fat **3g.**
Saturated fat **1g.**
Sodium **215mg.**

2 onions, sliced
2 celery stalks, sliced
¼ tsp. ground mace
½ tsp. fresh thyme, or ⅛ tsp. dried thyme leaves
1 bay leaf
freshly ground black pepper
5 cups fish stock or unsalted chicken stock
1 lb. fillet from a firm, white-fleshed fish, such as grouper, haddock or pollock, skinned and cut into 1-inch chunks
2 tbsp. farina
1½ lb. spinach, stemmed and washed
2 tbsp. heavy cream

Put the onions, celery, mace, thyme, bay leaf and some pepper into a large pot. Pour in 1 cup of the stock and bring the mixture to a boil. Cover the pot, reduce the heat to maintain a strong simmer, and cook the vegetables and seasonings for 30 minutes. Remove the lid and increase the heat to medium high. Cook the mixture until the liquid has evaporated and the onions are lightly browned — about 10 minutes more.

Meanwhile, pour the remaining 4 cups of stock into a large skillet over medium-high heat and bring it to a simmer. Add the fish chunks and poach them in the simmering stock until they are opaque and feel firm to the touch — about three minutes. Remove the fish pieces with a slotted spoon and set them aside; reserve the poaching liquid.

Transfer 1 cup of the poaching liquid to a small saucepan and bring it to a boil. Whisk in the farina and cook the liquid until it thickens — about four minutes. Set the liquid aside.

Pour the remaining poaching liquid into the pot containing the vegetables. Stir in the spinach and cook it over medium-high heat until it wilts — about four minutes. Purée the spinach mixture with the farina-thickened liquid in two batches in a blender, food processor or food mill. Return the soup to the pot over medium heat. Stir in the cream and the fish pieces, and cook the soup for two minutes. Serve immediately.

Shanghai Scallop Soup with 20 Garlic Cloves

Serves 4
Working (and total) time: about 40 minutes

Calories **230**
Protein **25g.**
Cholesterol **43mg.**
Total fat **3g.**
Saturated fat **1g.**
Sodium **355mg.**

1 lb. sea scallops, the bright white connective tissue removed, the larger scallops halved or quartered
2 tbsp. dry sherry
1 tbsp. low-sodium soy sauce
freshly ground black pepper
6 cups unsalted chicken stock
20 garlic cloves, peeled
8 oz. bok choy, the leaves cut into chiffonade (about 1½ cups), the stems sliced diagonally into ¼-inch pieces (about 1½ cups)
¼ cup fresh lemon juice
2 oz. cellophane (bean-thread) noodles, soaked in hot water for 20 minutes, drained and cut into 1-inch lengths
1 tbsp. chopped cilantro

Rinse the scallops under cold running water and drain them. Put the scallops into a bowl along with the sherry, soy sauce and some pepper. Gently stir the scallops to coat them with the marinade; then set the bowl aside while you prepare the soup.

Pour the stock into a large pot and bring it to a boil. Add the garlic cloves, reduce the heat and simmer the stock until the cloves are tender — about 15 minutes. Then stir in the bok choy leaves and stems, and simmer the soup for five minutes more.

Stir in the lemon juice, the noodles and the scallops with their marinade. Cook the soup until the scallops are opaque — about one minute. Stir in the cilantro and serve immediately.

Chilled Tomato-and-Shrimp Soup

Serves 4
Working time: about 20 minutes
Total time: about 1 hour and 20 minutes (includes chilling)

Calories **120**
Protein **14g.**
Cholesterol **97mg.**
Total fat **1g.**
Saturated fat **0g.**
Sodium **150mg.**

2 cups unsalted veal or chicken stock
4 ripe tomatoes, peeled, seeded and coarsely chopped
½ cucumber, peeled, seeded and coarsely chopped
1 scallion, trimmed and sliced into thin rounds
2 tbsp. red wine vinegar
¼ tsp. white pepper
1 tsp. Dijon mustard
4 to 8 drops hot red-pepper sauce
¾ lb. baby shrimp
½ cup croutons (optional; technique, page 9)

Pour the stock into a serving bowl. Stir in the tomatoes, cucumber, scallion, vinegar, pepper, mustard and red-pepper sauce. Add the shrimp and stir again. Cover the bowl and refrigerate it for at least one hour.

Serve the soup in chilled soup bowls; if you wish, garnish each portion with a few croutons.

Mussel and Artichoke Chowder

Serves 4
Working (and total) time: about 1 hour and 15 minutes

Calories **340**
Protein **21g.**
Cholesterol **82mg.**
Total fat **9g.**
Saturated fat **2g.**
Sodium **560mg.**

2 artichokes
juice of ½ lemon
1 cup dry white wine
24 mussels, scrubbed and debearded
1 tbsp. safflower oil
2 onions, finely diced (about 1½ cups)
2 tbsp. flour
2 cups fish stock
12 oz. boiling potatoes, finely diced (about 1¼ cups)
1 large carrot, finely diced (about ¾ cup)
1 bay leaf
1 fresh thyme sprig, or ¼ tsp. dried thyme leaves
¼ tsp. ground mace
¼ tsp. salt
⅛ tsp. white pepper
2 cups low-fat milk
1 tsp. paprika

To prepare the artichokes for cooking, first remove two or three layers of the outer leaves: Pull each leaf out and down until it snaps off at its base; stop when you reach the tender inner leaves. Cut off the top of the artichoke about 1½ inches above the base. Discard the outer leaves.

Cut off the stem flush with the base, then peel around the base in a spiral motion to pare away the dark green bases of the leaves. Turn the artichoke over. With the same spiral motion you used to cut off the leaf bases, trim the light green parts from the upper half of the artichoke. Using a sturdy teaspoon, scrape out the choke — the densely packed, fibrous center — and discard it. To preserve its color, drop the bottom into water mixed with the lemon juice. Prepare the other artichoke in the same way.

Pour the wine into a large, nonreactive pot over medium heat and bring it to a simmer. Add the mussels and cover the pot. Steam the mussels, shaking the pot a few times, until they open — about two minutes. Transfer the opened mussels to a bowl; discard any that remain closed. Reserve the wine.

Rinse the pot and heat the oil in it over medium heat. Add the onions and cook them, stirring, until they are ▶

translucent — about four minutes. Whisk in the flour, then the reserved wine, forming a paste. Slowly pour in the stock, whisking constantly. Bring the liquid to a boil and reduce the heat to maintain a simmer. Simmer the liquid until it is thickened — about five minutes.

Remove the mussels from their shells, working over a bowl to catch any of their juices. Line a sieve with cheesecloth and strain the juices through it into the onion mixture. Add the potatoes, carrot, bay leaf, thyme, mace, salt and pepper. Simmer the vegetables, partially covered, for about 10 minutes. Discard the bay leaf and the thyme sprig if you used it, and continue cooking the vegetables until the potatoes and car-

rot are tender — about five minutes more.

While the potatoes and carrot are cooking, pour 4 cups of water into a nonreactive saucepan. Bring the water to a boil and add the artichoke bottoms; reduce the heat and simmer the bottoms until they can be easily pierced through with the tip of a sharp knife — about 15 minutes. Drain the bottoms; when they are cool enough to handle, cut them into small dice.

Add the diced artichoke to the pot. Stir in the milk and the mussels, and cook the chowder over low heat until the mussels are heated through — three to four minutes. Sprinkle the chowder with the paprika just before serving.

Fish Soup
with Red-Pepper Sauce

Serves 6
Working (and total) time: about 45 minutes

Calories **205**
Protein **17g.**
Cholesterol **36mg.**
Total fat **9g.**
Saturated fat **1g.**
Sodium **160mg.**

6 cups fish stock
3 large leeks, trimmed, the green tops discarded, the white parts split, washed thoroughly to remove all grit, and thinly sliced
3 cups finely shredded Savoy cabbage (about 8 oz.)
2 ripe tomatoes, peeled, seeded and chopped
1 lb. fillet from a firm, white-fleshed fish such as cod, sable or sturgeon, rinsed and cut into 1-inch chunks
¼ cup freshly grated Romano cheese

Red-pepper sauce
2 whole-wheat bread slices, crusts removed
1 sweet red pepper, seeded, deribbed and chopped
2 large garlic cloves, chopped
⅛ tsp. cayenne pepper
3 tbsp. virgin olive oil

To prepare the red-pepper sauce, first put the bread slices into a bowl and pour in enough water to cover them. Soak the slices for 10 minutes, then squeeze out the water and transfer the bread to a food processor. Add the red pepper, garlic and cayenne pepper, and

purée the mixture. With the machine still running, dribble in the olive oil; the resulting sauce should be thick. Set the sauce aside.

For the soup, pour the stock into a large pot and bring it to a boil. Add the leeks, cabbage and tomatoes, then reduce the heat and simmer the vegetables until they are tender — about 10 minutes. Add the fish and cook the soup until the fish is firm and opaque — about three minutes. Pass the cheese and the red-pepper sauce in separate bowls.

Oyster Soup with Leeks

Serves 6
Working (and total) time: about 45 minutes

Calories **125**
Protein **8g.**
Cholesterol **52mg.**
Total fat **5g.**
Saturated fat **3g.**
Sodium **115mg.**

1 tbsp. unsalted butter
2 large leeks, trimmed, split, washed thoroughly to remove all grit, and thinly sliced
2 tsp. fresh thyme, or ½ tsp. dried thyme leaves
3 garlic cloves, finely chopped
½ cup dry white wine
2½ cups fish stock
⅛ tsp. salt
freshly ground black pepper
1 pint freshly shucked large oysters
¼ cup light cream

Melt the butter in a large, heavy-bottomed pot over medium-high heat. Add the leeks and thyme, then cover the pot and cook the leeks, stirring them several times, for 10 minutes.

Add the garlic and wine; continue cooking, stirring frequently, until the wine evaporates — about five minutes. Pour in the stock, then add the salt and some pepper, and simmer the mixture for 10 minutes.

While the stock is simmering, set aside 12 of the oysters. Purée the remaining oysters with their liquid in a food processor or blender.

Remove the pot from the heat, then whisk in the oyster purée and the cream. Set the pot over very low heat and cook the soup just long enough to heat it through — about three minutes. Place two of the reserved oysters in each of six heated soup plates. Pour the soup over the oysters and serve at once.

Hot and Sweet Soup with Seafood Dumplings

Serves 8
Working time: about 1 hour
Total time: about 1 hour and 15 minutes

Calories **135**
Protein **17g.**
Cholesterol **74mg.**
Total fat **3g.**
Saturated fat **1g.**
Sodium **240mg.**

8 oz. finely chopped lean pork
8 oz. medium shrimp, peeled, deveined if necessary, and finely chopped
8 oz. crab meat, picked over
2 scallions, trimmed and finely chopped
1½ tsp. finely chopped fresh ginger
1 egg white, beaten
8 cups unsalted chicken stock
2 tsp. sweet chili sauce, or 1 tsp. crushed hot red-pepper flakes mixed with 2 tsp. corn syrup and 1 tsp. vinegar
½ cup fresh lemon juice
1½ cups small cantaloupe balls
¼ tsp. salt

Combine the pork, shrimp, crab meat, scallions, ginger and egg white in a large bowl. Shape heaping tea-spoonfuls of the mixture into dumplings about 1 inch in diameter, moistening your palms from time to time to keep the mixture from sticking to them.

Pour the stock into a large pot and bring it to a boil. Reduce the heat to maintain a strong simmer and add the chili sauce or pepper-flake mixture and ¼ cup of the lemon juice. Gently drop half of the dumplings into the hot liquid and simmer them for five minutes. Remove the dumplings with a slotted spoon and set them aside. Drop the remaining dumplings into the liquid and simmer them for five minutes. When the second batch is done, return the first batch of dumplings to the pot. Heat the dumplings through, then add the melon balls, the salt and the remaining ¼ cup of lemon juice. Serve the soup in individual bowls.

A Fine Kettle of Fish

Serves 8
Working (and total) time: about 45 minutes

Calories **200**
Protein **25g.**
Cholesterol **94mg.**
Total fat **6g.**
Saturated fat **1g.**
Sodium **190mg.**

6 cups fish stock or unsalted chicken stock
1 cup dry white wine
2 tbsp. virgin olive oil
4 scallions, trimmed and finely chopped
16 littleneck clams, scrubbed
16 mussels, scrubbed and debearded
16 medium shrimp, peeled, deveined if necessary
1½ lb. Pacific red rockfish or red snapper fillets, cut into 1-inch cubes
3 large, ripe tomatoes (about 1½ lb.), peeled, seeded and coarsely chopped, or 14 oz. canned unsalted tomatoes, drained and coarsely chopped
3 tbsp. finely cut chives
1 tbsp. fresh thyme, or ¾ tsp. dried thyme leaves
grated zest of 1 lemon
⅛ tsp. cayenne pepper
⅛ tsp. crushed saffron threads
¼ cup finely chopped fresh parsley

Pour the stock, wine and oil into a large, nonreactive pot. Add the scallions and bring the liquid to a boil. Add the clams and mussels and cook them, partially covered, for two minutes. Remove the opened clams and mussels and set them aside. Partially cover the pot again and cook the mixture for two minutes more. Remove and set aside the opened clams and mussels; discard any that remain closed. Strain the cooking liquid into a bowl through a sieve lined with cheesecloth. Rinse the pot and return the strained liquid to it.

Add the shrimp and fish to the pot and return the liquid to a boil. Stir in the tomatoes, chives, thyme, lemon zest, cayenne pepper, saffron and parsley. Add the reserved clams and mussels and remove the pot from the heat. Let the soup stand for five minutes so that the flavors may meld.

To serve the soup, divide the clams, mussels and shrimp among eight bowls. Ladle some fish and broth into each bowl and serve at once.

Thai Shrimp Soup with Lemon Grass

Serves 6 as a first course
Working time: about 30 minutes
Total time: about 45 minutes

Calories **50**
Protein **6g.**
Cholesterol **38mg.**
Total fat **0g.**
Saturated fat **0g.**
Sodium **180mg.**

2 tsp. safflower oil
8 oz. small shrimp, peeled, deveined if necessary and halved lengthwise, the shells reserved
2½ cups unsalted chicken stock
2 stalks lemon grass, the root ends and woody tops trimmed off, the stalks cut into 1-inch-long pieces, or 1 tsp. grated lemon zest
¼ cup fresh lime juice
½ tsp. sambal oelek or crushed hot red-pepper flakes
2 tsp. fish sauce
6 paper-thin slices of lime for garnish
cilantro leaves for garnish (optional)

Heat the oil in a heavy-bottomed pot over medium heat. Add the shrimp shells and cook them, stirring, until they turn bright pink — about one minute. Add the stock, 2½ cups of water and the lemon grass if you are using it. (If you are substituting lemon zest, do not add it yet.) Bring the liquid to a boil, then reduce the heat to medium low, cover the pot, and simmer the mixture for five minutes. Turn off the heat and let the liquid stand for 15 minutes.

Strain the stock into a bowl. Discard the solids and return the liquid to the pot. Bring the liquid to a simmer and add the lime juice, crushed red pepper, fish sauce and shrimp. If you are using lemon zest, add it now. Cook the soup until the shrimp are opaque — about one minute. To serve, ladle the soup into bowls and garnish each one with a lime slice and, if you like, some cilantro leaves.

EDITOR'S NOTE: *Fish sauce is usually available in supermarkets; fresh lemon grass may be purchased in Asian grocery stores.*

Corn, Scallop and Fettuccine Soup

Serves 4
Working (and total) time: about 25 minutes

Calories **330**
Protein **21g.**
Cholesterol **43mg.**
Total fat **9g.**
Saturated fat **3g.**
Sodium **385mg.**

12 oz. sea scallops, the bright white connective tissue removed, the large scallops cut in half horizontally
⅛ tsp. white pepper
½ tsp. salt
1 cup low-fat milk
4 cups fish stock
4 oz. spinach fettuccine
⅔ cup fresh or frozen corn kernels
1 tbsp. safflower oil
1 tbsp. unsalted butter
2 tbsp. finely chopped shallot
½ cup dry white wine
½ tsp. chopped fresh thyme, or ⅛ tsp. dried thyme leaves

Rinse the scallops under cold running water and drain them. Season the scallops with the pepper and ¼ teaspoon of the salt, and set them aside.

Pour the milk and stock into a large pot. Sprinkle in the remaining ¼ teaspoon of salt and bring the liquid to a boil. Add the fettuccine and corn. Cover the pot until the liquid returns to a boil, then cook until the pasta is *al dente* — about eight minutes.

While the fettuccine and corn are cooking, heat the oil and butter together in a heavy-bottomed skillet over medium-high heat. Add the scallops and sauté them for 30 seconds on each side. Add the shallot and cook, stirring, for one minute. Pour in the wine, then add the thyme and cook for one minute more.

When the pasta is ready, combine it with the scallop mixture and serve at once.

Vietnamese Crab-and-Asparagus Soup

Serves 6
Working (and total) time: about 30 minutes

Calories **130**
Protein **16g.**
Cholesterol **59mg.**
Total fat **5g.**
Saturated fat **1g.**
Sodium **390mg.**

4 dried Asian mushrooms, covered with 1 cup of boiling water and soaked for 20 minutes
1 tbsp. safflower oil
3 scallions, trimmed, the white parts chopped, the green tops thinly sliced crosswise
3 garlic cloves, finely chopped
5 cups unsalted chicken stock
8 oz. fresh asparagus, trimmed and cut diagonally into 1-inch pieces
1 tbsp. fish sauce or low-sodium soy sauce
freshly ground black pepper
1 lb. crab meat, picked over
2 tbsp. chopped cilantro, plus several whole leaves for garnish

Strain the mushroom-soaking liquid through a fine sieve lined with cheesecloth and set the liquid aside. Cut off and discard the stems; slice the caps.

Heat the oil in a heavy-bottomed pot over medium-high heat. Add the white scallion parts and the garlic; sauté them, stirring often, for one minute. Pour in the mushroom-soaking liquid and the stock, then add the mushroom caps and bring the mixture to a boil. Add the asparagus, the fish sauce or soy sauce, the green scallion tops and some pepper. Return the liquid to a boil, then reduce the heat to maintain a simmer. Cook the asparagus pieces until they are barely tender — about three minutes.

Add the crab meat and stir in the chopped cilantro. Simmer the soup for two minutes more to heat the crab through. Garnish the soup with the cilantro leaves before serving.

Fruit soups, long savored in Middle Europe, can be a welcome addition to the menu. Here are three, made with pears, cantaloupe and orange, and peaches.

Golden Gazpacho

Serves 6 as a first course
Working time: about 15 minutes
Total time: about 1 hour and 15 minutes (includes chilling)

Calories **75**
Protein **3g.**
Cholesterol **1mg.**
Total fat **1g.**
Saturated fat **0g.**
Sodium **20mg.**

½ ripe cantaloupe, peeled, seeded and diced
2 garlic cloves, peeled
2 yellow peppers, seeded, deribbed and quartered
½ to 1 jalapeño pepper, seeded and deribbed (caution, page 95)
½ cup loosely packed cilantro leaves
1 navel orange, peeled and quartered, the peel of one quarter reserved
1 ½ cups fresh orange juice
3 scallions, trimmed, the green tops discarded
1 ½ tbsp. fresh lime juice
½ cup plain low-fat yogurt
12 cilantro leaves for garnish

Place all the ingredients except the yogurt in a food processor and purée the mixture. Add the yogurt and operate the machine in short bursts until the yogurt is mixed in. Transfer the soup to a bowl or jar, cover it tightly, and refrigerate it for at least one hour.

Garnish each serving with the cilantro leaves.

EDITOR'S NOTE: *In the event that yellow peppers cannot be found, use sweet red peppers instead.*

Gingery Pear Soup

Serves 4 as a first course
Working time: about 10 minutes
Total time: about 30 minutes

Calories **150**
Protein **4g.**
Cholesterol **6mg.**
Total fat **6g.**
Saturated fat **1g.**
Sodium **210mg.**

1 tbsp. safflower oil
2 tbsp. finely chopped fresh ginger
1 tbsp. finely chopped shallot
¼ cup pear brandy (optional)
1 lb. Bartlett pears (preferably red) quartered, cored and sliced into thin wedges
2 cups unsalted chicken stock
¼ tsp. salt
1 cup low-fat milk
4 parsley sprigs for garnish

Heat the oil in a large, heavy-bottomed pot over medium heat. Add the ginger and shallot and cook them, stirring, until the shallot is translucent — two to three minutes. Pour in the brandy if you are using it, and cook the mixture until the liquid is nearly evaporated — about three minutes more.

Add the pears, stock and salt. Reduce the heat and simmer the mixture, partially covered, until the pears are translucent and soft — 15 to 20 minutes. Remove a few pear slices and set them aside for garnish.

Purée the contents of the pot in a food processor or blender. Return the purée to the pot, stir in the milk and warm the soup over low heat, taking care that it does not boil. Serve the soup immediately, garnished with the reserved pear slices and the parsley sprigs.

Peach Soup Flambé

Serves 4 as a first course or dessert
Working (and total) time: about 1 hour

Calories **185**
Protein **2g.**
Cholesterol **5mg.**
Total fat **3g.**
Saturated fat **2g.**
Sodium **6mg.**

2 lb. ripe peaches or nectarines, washed
¼ cup fresh lemon juice
1 tbsp. honey
1 tsp. chopped fresh rosemary, or ¼ tsp. dried rosemary
4 tsp. sugar
4 tbsp. sour cream
3 tbsp. Cognac or Armagnac

Pour 2 quarts of water into a large pot. Bring the water to a boil, then add the peaches and cook them until their skins loosen — 5 to 15 minutes, depending on their ripeness. Using a slotted spoon, remove the peaches and set them aside to cool. Pour off all but 1½ cups of the cooking water.

When the peaches are cool enough to handle, peel them, then cut them in half and remove the pits. Discard the skins and pits; return the peach halves to the pot. Add the lemon juice, honey, rosemary and 3 teaspoons of the sugar, and bring the mixture to a boil. Reduce the heat and simmer the peaches, stirring frequently, for 15 minutes.

Purée the mixture in batches in a blender, a food processor or a food mill. Pour the purée back into the pot and reheat it slowly over low heat, stirring occasionally, for about 10 minutes. Stir in 2 tablespoons of the sour cream.

Transfer the soup to a warmed serving bowl. Mix the remaining 2 tablespoons of sour cream with the remaining teaspoon of sugar, then spoon the mixture onto the center of the soup. Gently spoon the Cognac or Armagnac around the sour cream, taking care that the brandy floats on the surface of the soup. Dim the lights, ignite the brandy, and serve the soup with the flames dancing.

2 *Asian inspired, this beef stew with water chestnuts and butternut squash takes its character from the tangerine juice and peel it includes (recipe, page 101).*

Stew's Ever-Constant Magic

Is there anything so simple or so nourishing as a stew? Conjuring up the memory of a Provençal beef stew simmering on his grandmother's kitchen stove, French author Pierre Huguenin recalled that it sounded "like a little bubbling spring" as it cooked. "Since midday," he wrote, "it had been murmuring gently, giving out sweet smells. Thyme, rosemary, bay leaves, spices, the wine of the marinade and the meat were becoming transformed under the magic wand which is the fire, into a delicious whole."

In the alchemy that is stew making, almost any ingredient can be transmuted into something special. This section endeavors to delight by presenting a broad repertoire of stews based on vegetables, fish and meat. Some of the recipes bear a down-home touch: The rabbit stew on page 105, for example, celebrates its Southern roots through the inclusion of corn, lima beans and potatoes. Other dishes have cosmopolitan flavor, announcing their debt to ethnic cuisines by calling for spices and seasonings in exotic combinations: The Java lamb curry on page 99 draws on ginger, cloves, sweet red pepper and tamarind to give it the savor of the tropical island that inspired it. The flounder curry on page 125 features the turmeric, cardamom and mace characteristic of Indian cooking.

Wherever fattier cuts of meat are called for, the stews are degreased; when lean cuts are used, the preparation times are pared back to guarantee succulence — abbreviating, in the bargain, the cook's time in the kitchen. The sauerbraten stew with candied ginger on page 113 not only uses lean beef but shortcuts the marinating time of traditional sauerbraten by at least two days. The beef is cut up in small pieces and sautéed with the ginger; a hot marinade is then poured over all. Because the pieces present multiple surfaces, they need only brief steaming to absorb flavor.

During the time it simmers, a stew may be left practically unattended, freeing the cook to prepare the rest of the meal. In the meantime, as the liquid in the pot reduces, it works a final bit of magic, turning itself into a sauce that demands no further sorcery but to be skimmed of any surface fat before serving.

Sherried Vegetable Potpourri

Serves 6
Working time: about 30 minutes
Total time: about 1 hour

Calories **115**
Protein **3g.**
Cholesterol **0mg.**
Total fat **3g.**
Saturated fat **0g.**
Sodium **165mg.**

1 tbsp. safflower oil
¼ cup thinly sliced shallots
2 garlic cloves, finely chopped
1 cup dry sherry
1 tbsp. chopped fresh thyme, or ¾ tsp. dried thyme leaves
1 carrot, cut into ¾-inch pieces
1 small rutabaga, peeled and cut into ¾-inch cubes
1½ cups cauliflower florets
1 small yellow squash, halved lengthwise and cut into ¾-inch-thick pieces
1 small zucchini, halved lengthwise and cut into ¾-inch-thick pieces
1 small eggplant, cut into ¾-inch cubes
1 sweet red pepper, seeded, deribbed and cut into ¾-inch squares
14 oz. canned unsalted tomatoes, seeded and coarsely chopped, with their juice
½ cup coarsely shredded red cabbage
1 tsp. celery seeds
⅜ tsp. salt
freshly ground black pepper

Pour the oil into a large, heavy-bottomed pot over medium heat. Cook the shallots in the hot oil, stirring frequently, until they are golden — about seven minutes. Add the garlic and continue cooking for one minute. Pour in all but 1 tablespoon of the sherry; add the thyme and bring the mixture to a boil, then cook it for two minutes more.

Put a steamer into a large saucepan or pot; pour in about 2 cups of water and bring it to a boil. Add the carrot, rutabaga and cauliflower and steam them, covered, for seven minutes. Add the yellow squash, zucchini, eggplant and red pepper; steam these for three minutes more. Transfer the steamed vegetables to the pot containing the shallots; do not discard the liquid.

Add ½ cup of the liquid to the pot along with the tomatoes and their juice. Stir in the red cabbage, celery seeds, salt and some pepper; bring the stew to a simmer and cook it, uncovered, for 10 minutes. Stir in the reserved tablespoon of sherry just before serving.

Vegetable Stew with Okra

Serves 4
Working time: about 25 minutes
Total time: about 45 minutes

Calories **195**
Protein **5g.**
Cholesterol **0mg.**
Total fat **8g.**
Saturated fat **1g.**
Sodium **115mg.**

2 tbsp. safflower oil
1 large sweet red pepper, seeded, deribbed and cut into ¾-inch squares
12 oz. pearl onions, peeled and trimmed (about 2 cups)
2 garlic cloves, finely chopped
2 cups unsalted vegetable or chicken stock
1 small eggplant (about ¾ lb.), cut into ¾-inch cubes
1 yellow squash, cut into ¾-inch chunks
4 oz. fresh okra (8 to 10 pods), washed and sliced into ¾-inch-thick rounds
1½ lb. ripe tomatoes, peeled, seeded and coarsely chopped, or 14 oz. canned unsalted tomatoes, chopped, with their juice
½ small butternut squash, peeled, seeded and julienned (about 1½ cups)
1½ tbsp. chopped fresh basil, or 2 tbsp. dried basil
2 tsp. Dijon mustard
1 tsp. paprika, preferably Hungarian
⅛ tsp. salt
freshly ground black pepper
cayenne pepper

Heat 1 tablespoon of the safflower oil in a large, heavy-bottomed pot over medium heat. Add the red pepper and pearl onions and cook them, stirring occasionally, until the pepper begins to soften and the onions have colored slightly — about five minutes. Stir in the garlic and cook for 30 seconds. Pour in the stock and bring it to a brisk simmer. Reduce the heat and simmer the vegetables for 10 minutes.

While the vegetables are simmering, heat the remaining tablespoon of oil in a large, heavy-bottomed skillet over medium-high heat. Add the eggplant, yellow squash and okra, and sauté them until they begin to soften — about three minutes. Stir in the tomatoes, butternut squash and basil, and cook them for three minutes. Add this mixture to the vegetables simmering in the pot. Stir in the mustard, paprika, salt, some black pepper and a pinch of cayenne pepper. Cook the stew until all of the vegetables are tender — about five minutes. Serve at once.

Sweet Potato Stew

Serves 6 as a side dish
Working time: about 40 minutes
Total time: about 1 hour

Calories **235**
Protein **5g.**
Cholesterol **11mg.**
Total fat **5g.**
Saturated fat **3g.**
Sodium **340mg.**

3 sweet potatoes (1½ to 2 lb.)
2 tbsp. unsalted butter
¼ cup finely chopped shallot
1 tsp. mustard seeds
1 small rutabaga (about 12 oz.), peeled, sliced ½ inch thick and cut into 1-inch squares
2 young turnips (about 8 oz.), peeled, sliced ½ inch thick and cut into 1-inch squares
12 oz. celeriac, peeled, sliced ½ inch thick and cut into 1-inch squares
3 cups unsalted veal, chicken or vegetable stock
2 tbsp. fresh lemon juice
½ tsp. salt
2 cups loosely packed parsley sprigs (about 1 bunch)

Preheat the oven to 400° F. Prick each sweet potato with a fork. Bake the sweet potatoes until they are tender — about 45 minutes.

Meanwhile, melt the butter in a large, nonreactive, heavy-bottomed pot over medium-low heat. Stir in the shallot and mustard seeds, and cook them for one minute. Add the rutabaga, turnips and celeriac; continue cooking, stirring frequently, for 10 minutes. Pour in 1½ cups of the stock and the lemon juice; sprinkle in ¼ teaspoon of the salt. Bring the mixture to a boil, cover the pot and set it aside.

When the sweet potatoes are cooked, halve them lengthwise and spoon their flesh into a food processor or blender (eat the skins if you like). Purée the potatoes with the remaining 1½ cups of stock and the remaining ¼ teaspoon of salt. Stir the purée and the parsley sprigs into the mixture in the pot. Cook the stew over medium-low heat until the parsley is wilted and the stew is heated through — about three minutes.

Vegetable Stew, East Indian Style

Serves 6
Working time: about 1½ hours
Total time: about 2 hours

Calories **295**
Protein **16g.**
Cholesterol **8mg.**
Total fat **13g.**
Saturated fat **3g.**
Sodium **330mg.**

1 tbsp. safflower oil
1 tbsp. unsalted butter
1 tbsp. finely chopped fresh ginger
1 medium onion, thinly sliced
2 bunches of scallions, trimmed and cut diagonally into 2-inch lengths
3 garlic cloves, thinly sliced
1 tsp. crushed saffron threads
½ tsp. ground cardamom
½ tsp. ground cumin
½ tsp. ground cinnamon
¼ tsp. salt
freshly ground black pepper
8 cups unsalted chicken or vegetable stock
2 boiling potatoes, scrubbed and cut into ½-inch pieces
6 celery stalks, julienned
2 carrots, julienned
4 tsp. cornstarch
2 cups firmly packed stemmed collard greens, chopped
2 cups firmly packed stemmed kale, chopped
2 cups firmly packed stemmed mustard greens, chopped
1 lb. firm tofu (bean curd), cut into 1-inch cubes
¼ cup unsalted pistachios, shelled and chopped
Cucumber-yogurt sauce
¼ cup plain low-fat yogurt
1 cucumber, peeled, seeded and finely chopped
1 ripe tomato, peeled, seeded and finely chopped
1 tbsp. chopped onion
2 tbsp. chopped cilantro
⅛ tsp. salt
¼ tsp. ground cumin

To prepare the sauce, combine the yogurt, cucumber, tomato, onion, cilantro, salt and cumin in a bowl. Cover the bowl with plastic wrap and refrigerate it.

Heat the oil and butter in a large, heavy-bottomed pot over medium heat. Add the ginger and cook, stirring, for one minute. Add the onion and scallions, cover the pot, and cook, stirring occasionally, for five minutes. Add the garlic, saffron, cardamom, cumin, cinnamon, salt and a generous grinding of pepper; cook the mixture, stirring constantly, for two minutes.

Pour in all but ½ cup of the stock and add the potatoes. Simmer the stew, covered, for 10 minutes. Add the celery and carrots, and continue simmering until the potatoes are tender — 10 to 15 minutes. Mix the cornstarch with the remaining ½ cup of stock and stir the mixture into the stew. Simmer the stew until it thickens — about three minutes.

Stir in the collard greens, kale and mustard greens, and simmer the stew until the greens are tender — five to eight minutes more. Add the tofu; pass the yogurt sauce and pistachios separately. Serve immediately.

Chunky Beef Chili

Serves 8
Working time: about 1 hour
Total time: about 4 hours

Calories **230**
Protein **27g.**
Cholesterol **75mg.**
Total fat **10g.**
Saturated fat **3g.**
Sodium **460mg.**

2 dried ancho chili peppers, stemmed, seeded and quartered
2 jalapeño peppers, stemmed, seeded and coarsely chopped (caution, page 95)
2 tbsp. safflower oil
2 lb. beef chuck, trimmed of fat and cut into ½-inch chunks
2 large onions, finely chopped
2 celery stalks, finely chopped
2 garlic cloves, finely chopped
2 tbsp. finely chopped fresh ginger
1 tbsp. ground cumin
1 tbsp. Mexican oregano
¼ tsp. cayenne pepper
¼ tsp. freshly ground black pepper
1 tbsp. flour
14 oz. canned unsalted tomatoes, coarsely chopped, with their juice
1 bay leaf
1½ tsp. salt
½ tsp. grated orange zest

Put the ancho chilies into a small saucepan; pour in 2 cups of water and boil the liquid for five minutes. Turn off the heat and let the chilies soften for five minutes.

Transfer the chilies to a blender or food processor with ½ cup of their soaking liquid; reserve the remaining liquid. Add the jalapeño peppers and purée the chilies until the mixture is very smooth. Strain the purée through a sieve into the reserved soaking liquid, rubbing the solids through with a spoon.

Heat ½ tablespoon of the oil in a large, nonstick or heavy-bottomed skillet over medium-high heat. Add about one fourth of the beef chunks and cook them, turning the pieces frequently, until they are browned all over — approximately eight minutes. Transfer the browned beef to a large, heavy-bottomed pot. Brown the rest of the meat the same way, using all but ½ tablespoon of the remaining oil in the process.

Add the last ½ tablespoon of oil to the skillet along with the onions, celery and garlic. Saute the vegetables for five minutes, stirring frequently. Stir in the ginger, cumin, oregano, cayenne pepper and black pepper, and cook the mixture for one minute. Add the flour and cook for one minute more, stirring constantly. Transfer the mixture to the pot.

Pour the reserved chili mixture and 2 cups of water into the pot. Stir in the tomatoes and their juice along with the bay leaf, salt and orange zest. Cook the mixture, uncovered, over very low heat until the meat is tender — two and one half to three hours. (Do not allow the mixture to boil or the meat will toughen.) If the chili begins to get too thick, add water, ½ cup at a time, until it reaches the desired consistency.

EDITOR'S NOTE: *Black beans make an excellent accompaniment to this orange-scented chili.*

Chilies — A Cautionary Note

Both dried and fresh hot chilies should be handled with care. Their flesh and seeds contain volatile oils that can make skin tingle and cause eyes to burn. Rubber gloves offer protection — but the cook should still be careful not to touch the face, lips or eyes when working with chilies.

Soaking fresh chilies in cold, salted water for an hour will remove some of their fire. If canned chilies are substituted for fresh ones, they should be rinsed in cold water in order to eliminate as much of the brine used to preserve them as possible.

Lentil-Sausage Stew

Serves 6
Working time: about 15 minutes
Total time: about 1 hour

Calories **185**
Protein **12g.**
Cholesterol **12mg.**
Total fat **6g.**
Saturated fat **2g.**
Sodium **515mg.**

3 oz. chorizo sausage, skinned, sliced into very thin rounds, all but 8 of the rounds cut into thin strips
1 large onion, very finely chopped
1½ cups lentils, picked over
3 cups unsalted brown or chicken stock
1 large carrot, sliced into thin rounds
2 celery stalks, thinly sliced
1 tbsp. chopped fresh basil, or 2 tsp. dried basil
½ tsp. salt
freshly ground black pepper

Cook the chorizo rounds and strips in a large, heavy-bottomed pot over medium-low heat for three minutes. Remove the rounds and set them aside. Add the onion and continue cooking until the onion is translucent — about six minutes.

Rinse the lentils under cold running water and add them to the pot along with the stock and 3 cups of water. Bring the liquid to a simmer and cook the mixture, covered, until the lentils are soft — about 35 minutes. Add the carrot, celery, basil, salt and some pepper; simmer the stew, covered, until the carrot rounds are tender — seven to 10 minutes. Garnish the stew with the reserved chorizo rounds; serve at once.

Turkey Stew with Mediterranean Vegetables

Serves 4
Working time: about 40 minutes
Total time: about 2 hours

Calories **335**
Protein **33g.**
Cholesterol **85mg.**
Total fat **15g.**
Saturated fat **3g.**
Sodium **225mg.**

3 turkey drumsticks (about 2 lb.)
2 onions, sliced
1 whole garlic bulb, cut in half horizontally
1 tsp. fresh thyme, or ¼ tsp. dried thyme leaves
1 bay leaf
1 large eggplant (about 1 lb.), sliced into ½-inch-thick rounds, each round cut into 8 wedges
2 tbsp. virgin olive oil
3 medium zucchini (about 1 lb.), trimmed and sliced into 1-inch-thick rounds, the rounds halved
1 tbsp. chopped fresh oregano or parsley

Red-pepper sauce

1 sweet red pepper, seeded and coarsely chopped
4 garlic cloves, crushed
1 tbsp. chopped fresh oregano, or 1 tsp. dried oregano
¼ tsp. salt

Put the drumsticks, onions, garlic-bulb halves, thyme and bay leaf into a large pot. Pour in enough water (about 8 cups) to cover the ingredients; bring the liquid to a boil over medium-high heat. Cover the pot with the lid slightly ajar, then reduce the heat and simmer the stew until the turkey is tender — about one hour.

While the turkey is cooking, prepare the eggplant. Preheat the oven to 450° F. In a baking dish, toss the eggplant with the oil to coat the pieces. Bake the eggplant until it is lightly browned — about 15 minutes. Set the eggplant aside while you prepare the sauce.

Transfer ½ cup of the simmering broth to a small saucepan over medium-low heat. Add the red pepper, bring the liquid to a simmer, and cover the pan. Cook the pepper until it is tender — seven to eight minutes. Put the pepper pieces and broth in a blender along with the garlic, oregano and salt. Purée the mixture until a smooth sauce results. Return the sauce to the pan and set it aside.

When the turkey is tender, remove the drumsticks from the broth and set them aside. Cook the broth over high heat until only about 2 cups of liquid remain — 15 to 20 minutes.

While the broth is reducing, remove the meat from the drumsticks; discard the skin and tendons. Cut the meat into 1-inch pieces and set them aside.

Strain the reduced broth through a fine sieve into a bowl. Discard the solids; then degrease the broth *(box, page 55)*.

Return the broth to the pot and bring it to a boil. Add the zucchini, cover the pot and cook the zucchini until it is tender — about five minutes. Add the turkey pieces, eggplant and oregano or parsley; continue cooking the stew just long enough to heat them through. Reheat the sauce. Ladle the stew into deep plates and garnish each portion with a dollop of the sauce before serving.

Chicken Gumbo

Serves 6
Working time: about 35 minutes
Total time: about 1 hour and 10 minutes

Calories **295**
Protein **29g.**
Cholesterol **81mg.**
Total fat **12g.**
Saturated fat **3g.**
Sodium **315mg.**

1 tbsp. finely chopped garlic
1 tbsp. chopped fresh thyme, or ¾ tsp. dried thyme leaves
1 tsp. dry mustard
½ tsp. salt
½ tsp. paprika, preferably Hungarian
½ tsp. cracked black peppercorns
12 oz. chicken breast meat, cut crosswise into ½-inch-wide strips
12 oz. chicken thigh meat, cut into ½-inch-wide strips
juice of 1 lemon
1 tbsp. unsalted butter
1 large onion, sliced
5 celery stalks, cut lengthwise into ¼-inch strips, each strip cut into 1-inch-long bâtonnets
1½ tbsp. flour
2½ lb. ripe tomatoes, peeled, seeded and chopped, or 28 oz. canned unsalted tomatoes, drained and chopped
2 bay leaves
1 tbsp. olive oil
8 oz. okra, trimmed and cut into 1-inch lengths
2 cups unsalted chicken stock
1 sweet red pepper, seeded, deribbed and cut lengthwise into ¼-inch-wide strips
1 green pepper, seeded, deribbed and cut lengthwise into ¼-inch-wide strips

Mix the garlic with the thyme, mustard, salt, paprika and pepper. Toss the chicken strips with one third of the spice mixture and the lemon juice. Set the chicken aside to marinate at room temperature while you prepare the vegetables.

Melt the butter in a large, heavy-bottomed pot over medium-high heat. Add the onion and the celery bâtonnets, and sauté them, stirring frequently, until the onions are translucent — about eight minutes. Stir in the flour and the remaining two thirds of the spice mixture; continue cooking for two minutes more. Add the tomatoes and bay leaves. Reduce the heat and simmer the mixture for 15 minutes.

Meanwhile, heat the olive oil in a large, heavy-bottomed skillet over medium-high heat. Add the okra and sauté it, stirring frequently, until the pieces are well browned — about five minutes. Set the okra aside.

Add the marinated chicken strips, the stock and peppers to the tomato mixture. Simmer the stew for 20 minutes more, stirring several times.

Before serving, stir the okra into the stew and allow it to heat through.

EDITOR'S NOTE: *Rice pilaf makes an excellent foil for gumbo.*

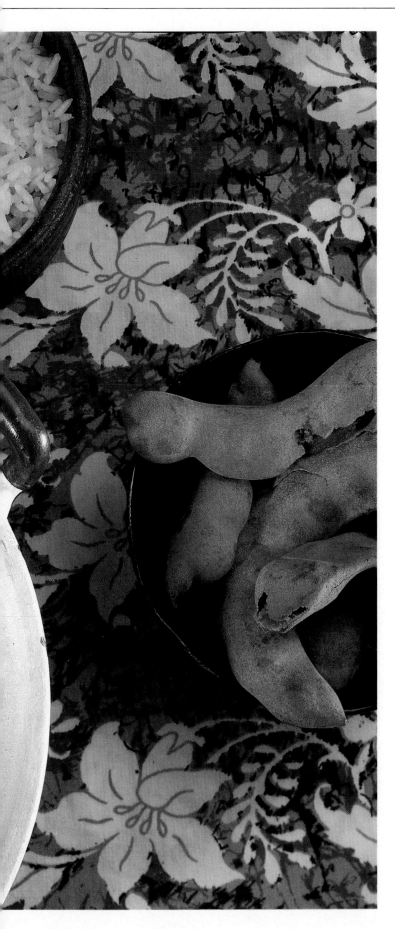

Java Lamb Curry
with Tamarind

Serves 4
Working time: about 30 minutes
Total time: about 1 hour and 30 minutes

Calories **375**
Protein **24g.**
Cholesterol **54mg.**
Total fat **24g.**
Saturated fat **13g.**
Sodium **380mg.**

1 lb. lean, boneless lamb (preferably leg or shoulder), cut into 1-inch cubes
1 tbsp. ground coriander
2 tsp. ground cumin
¼ tsp. crushed hot red-pepper flakes or chili paste
½ tsp. freshly ground black pepper
1 tbsp. flour
1 tbsp. safflower oil
1 large onion, chopped
1 sweet red pepper, seeded, deribbed and chopped
1 tbsp. finely chopped fresh ginger
2 garlic cloves, finely chopped
2 cups unsalted brown stock
¼ cup tamarind pulp, steeped in ½ cup boiling water for 10 minutes, the liquid strained and reserved
⅓ cup unsweetened coconut milk
½ tsp. salt
⅛ tsp. ground cinnamon
⅛ tsp. ground cloves
1 lemon, the zest julienned, the juice reserved
2 cups cauliflower florets
1 lemon (optional), sliced into thin rounds

Toss the lamb cubes with the coriander, cumin, red-pepper flakes, black pepper and flour. Heat the oil in a large, heavy-bottomed pot over medium-high heat. Add the lamb cubes and sauté them, in several batches if necessary, until they are browned on all sides — about eight minutes per batch. Stir in the onion, red pepper, ginger and garlic. Reduce the heat to medium; cover the pot and cook the mixture, stirring frequently to keep the onions from burning, for eight minutes.

Add the stock, tamarind liquid, coconut milk, salt, cinnamon and cloves. Bring the mixture to a simmer, then reduce the heat so that the liquid barely trembles; cover the pot and cook the mixture for 45 minutes.

Stir in the lemon zest, lemon juice and cauliflower. Continue to simmer the curry, covered, until the cauliflower is tender — about 15 minutes. If you like, garnish the curry with the lemon slices before serving.

EDITOR'S NOTE: *Tamarind pulp — the peeled, pitted, compressed flesh of a tropical plant native to India — is available in many markets, including those specializing in Indian and Mexican foods.*

If canned or frozen unsweetened coconut milk is not available, the coconut milk may be made at home: Mix ⅓ cup of unsweetened dried coconut in a blender with ⅓ cup of very hot water, then strain the liquid.

Chicken Stew with Zucchini and Tomatoes

Serves 4
Working time: about 35 minutes
Total time: about one hour

Calories **325**
Protein **32g.**
Cholesterol **66mg.**
Total fat **6g.**
Saturated fat **1g.**
Sodium **420mg.**

2½ lb. ripe tomatoes, peeled, seeded and chopped, or 28 oz. canned unsalted tomatoes, coarsely chopped, with their juice
1½ cups unsalted chicken stock
1 tsp. sugar
2 garlic cloves, finely chopped
1 tsp. dried basil
½ to ¾ tsp. chili powder
½ tsp. salt
freshly ground black pepper
2 chicken breast halves, skinned
3 oz. wide egg noodles (about 1½ cups)
2 zucchini (about 8 oz.), trimmed and cut into ½-inch-thick rounds

Put the tomatoes, stock, sugar, garlic, basil, chili powder, salt and some pepper into a large, heavy-bottomed pot over medium heat. Bring the liquid to a simmer and cook the mixture for 10 minutes.

Add the chicken breasts to the pot and poach them for 12 minutes. With a slotted spoon, remove the breasts — they will still be slightly undercooked — and set them aside.

Cook the noodles in 6 cups of boiling water with ¾ teaspoon of salt for three minutes. Drain the noodles well, then add them to the stew along with the zucchini rounds. When the chicken breasts are cool enough to handle, remove the meat from the bones. Cut the meat into ½-inch pieces and return it to the pot. Continue cooking the stew until the zucchini are tender — about five minutes more. Serve immediately.

Tangerine Beef Stew

Serves 4
Working time: about 40 minutes
Total time: about 2 hours and 30 minutes

Calories **595**
Protein **29g.**
Cholesterol **69mg.**
Total fat **17g.**
Saturated fat **4g.**
Sodium **380mg.**

3 tbsp. safflower oil
1 lb. boneless beef shin (sold as cross-cut shank) or other stew beef, trimmed of all fat and cut into 1-inch cubes
½ tbsp. Chinese five-spice powder
1 tbsp. flour
1 garlic clove, finely chopped
2 tsp. finely chopped fresh ginger
2 leeks, trimmed, the green tops discarded, the white parts split, washed thoroughly to remove all grit, and thinly sliced (about 1½ cups)
1 cup red wine
2 cups unsalted brown stock
3 strips tangerine zest, each about 2 inches long and 1 inch wide, pinned together with 1 whole clove
¼ cup fresh tangerine juice
1 cup fresh water chestnuts, peeled and sliced, or 1 cup canned water chestnuts, drained, rinsed and sliced
1 lb. butternut squash, peeled, seeded and cut into rectangles about 1½ inches long, ¾-inch wide and ¼-inch thick
½ tsp. salt
1 cup rice
2 tbsp. julienned tangerine zest (optional), blanched

Pour 2 tablespoons of the oil into a heavy-bottomed pot over medium-high heat. Sprinkle the beef cubes with the five-spice powder and the flour and toss them to coat them evenly. Add as many beef cubes to the oil as will fit in a single layer without touching. Brown the meat well on one side, then turn the pieces and continue cooking them, turning as necessary, until they are browned on all sides. Use a slotted spoon to transfer the beef to a plate, then cook any remaining cubes.

Pour off any oil remaining in the pot and clean the pot. Reduce the heat to low and pour in the last tablespoon of oil. Add the garlic, ginger and leeks, and cook them, stirring often, for five minutes. Return the beef cubes to the pot. Add the wine, stock, tangerine-zest strips and tangerine juice. Cover the pot and gently simmer the stew for one and one half hours.

Add the water chestnuts, squash and salt, and continue simmering the stew until the squash is tender — about 20 minutes. While the water chestnuts and squash are cooking, cook the rice. Spoon the stew over the rice; garnish it, if you like, with the julienned zest.

EDITOR'S NOTE: *This recipe works equally well when lamb shanks or veal shanks are used in place of the beef. A root vegetable such as carrot, sweet potato or turnip may be substituted for the squash. A variation of Chinese five-spice powder may be made at home by chopping in a blender equal parts Sichuan peppercorns, fennel seeds, ground cloves and ground cinnamon.*

Veal Stew
with Red, Green and
Yellow Peppers

Serves 4
Working time: about 30 minutes
Total time: about 2 hours

Calories **255**
Protein **22g.**
Cholesterol **69mg.**
Total fat **12g.**
Saturated fat **4g.**
Sodium **230mg.**

1 tbsp. safflower oil
1 lb. trimmed veal breast, cut into 1-inch chunks
2 onions, chopped
2 tsp. fresh thyme, or ½ tsp. dried thyme leaves
4 garlic cloves, finely chopped
1½ cups unsalted veal or chicken stock
½ cup dry white wine
¼ tsp. salt
freshly ground black pepper

1 sweet red pepper, seeded, deribbed and thinly sliced
1 green pepper, seeded, deribbed and thinly sliced
1 yellow pepper, seeded, deribbed and thinly sliced

Heat the safflower oil in a large, heavy-bottomed pot over medium-high heat. Add the veal chunks and sauté them, turning frequently, until they are lightly browned — about five minutes. Remove the veal and set it aside.

Add the onions and thyme to the pot and cook them until the onions are translucent — about four minutes. Stir in the garlic, then return the veal to the pot. Add the stock, wine, salt and some black pepper. Reduce the heat and simmer the stew, covered, until the veal is tender — about one hour and 15 minutes. At the end of the cooking time, degrease the liquid *(box, page 55)*.

Add the peppers and simmer the stew, covered, for a final 15 minutes. Serve immediately.

Rabbit Stew with Prunes

Serves 4
Working time: about 40 minutes
Total time: about 3 hours

Calories **355**
Protein **30g.**
Cholesterol **62mg.**
Total fat **14g.**
Saturated fat **4g.**
Sodium **230mg.**

one 2½-lb. rabbit, cut into serving pieces
1 cup red wine
1 bouquet garni, made by tying together 2 fresh thyme sprigs, several parsley stems and 1 bay leaf (if fresh thyme is unavailable, tie up ½ tsp. of dried thyme leaves in a piece of cheesecloth with the other herbs)
1 onion, chopped
1 carrot, chopped
4 garlic cloves, chopped
freshly ground black pepper
flour for dredging (about ¼ cup)
1 tbsp. safflower oil
1 tbsp. unsalted butter
¼ tsp. salt
2 cups unsalted chicken stock
20 pitted prunes (about 6 oz.)

Put the rabbit pieces into a large, nonreactive bowl with the wine, bouquet garni, onion, carrot, garlic and some pepper. Marinate the rabbit at room temperature for two hours, turning the pieces every now and then. Remove the rabbit pieces from the marinade and pat them dry with paper towels. Dredge the pieces in the flour so that they are lightly coated. Strain the marinade through a fine sieve into a bowl, reserving the vegetables and the liquid separately.

Heat the oil and butter together in a large, heavy-bottomed pot over medium-high heat. Add the rabbit pieces and sauté them, sprinkling them with the salt as they cook, until they are browned on each side — three to four minutes per side. Transfer the pieces to a plate.

Add the reserved onion, garlic and carrot to the pot. Sauté the vegetables, stirring constantly, until the onion is translucent — about four minutes. Pour in the strained marinade, then the stock; return the rabbit pieces to the pot. Bring the liquid to a boil, cover the pot, and reduce the heat to maintain a simmer; braise the rabbit for 30 minutes.

Add the prunes and again cover the pot; continue simmering the stew until the rabbit feels tender when pierced with a fork — about 20 minutes. With a slotted spoon, transfer the rabbit and prunes to a heated serving dish and keep them warm. Increase the heat to medium high and reduce the sauce until it is thick enough to coat the back of a spoon — about five minutes. Pour the sauce over the rabbit and prunes, and serve at once. If you like, serve a dish of lightly buttered noodles alongside.

EDITOR'S NOTE: *The amount of time required to stew rabbit varies widely; if you are using a large rabbit, the time may have to be doubled.*

Rabbit Stew with Sherry

THIS RECIPE WAS INSPIRED BY THE SOUTH'S CLASSIC
BRUNSWICK STEW, WHICH USES SQUIRREL. DINERS ARE
ENCOURAGED TO PLUCK THE MEAT AND CORN FROM
THE STEW AND EAT THEM WITH THEIR FINGERS.

Serves 4
Working time: about 45 minutes
Total time: about 1 hour

Calories **520**
Protein **36g.**
Cholesterol **62mg.**
Total fat **15g.**
Saturated fat **4g.**
Sodium **365mg.**

½ tsp. salt
1 small rabbit (about 2½ lb.), cut into 8 serving pieces
¼ cup flour
2 tsp. paprika, preferably Hungarian
1 tsp. chopped fresh thyme, or ¼ tsp. dried thyme leaves
⅛ tsp. freshly ground black pepper
1½ tbsp. safflower oil
1 onion, cut into chunks
1 garlic clove, finely chopped
1 cup dry sherry
2 cups unsalted chicken stock
1 large ripe tomato, peeled, seeded and coarsely chopped
1 lb. red potatoes, washed and sliced into ½-inch-thick rounds
2 small ears of corn, each cut into 6 rounds
1½ cups fresh lima beans, or 1 cup frozen baby lima beans, thawed under hot running water

Sprinkle ¼ teaspoon of the salt over the rabbit pieces. Combine the flour, paprika, thyme and pepper in a bowl, and dredge the pieces in the mixture. Heat 1 tablespoon of the safflower oil in a shallow, heavy-bottomed pot over medium heat. Add the pieces and cook them until they are brown — about two minutes per side. Remove the rabbit and set it aside.

Add the remaining ½ tablespoon of the oil to the pot; then add the onion and cook, stirring frequently, until it is translucent — about four minutes. Add the garlic and continue cooking for 30 seconds. Return the rabbit pieces to the pot and pour in the sherry. Cook the mixture until the sherry is reduced by two thirds — four to five minutes. Add the stock and tomato, and bring the liquid to a boil. Reduce the heat and simmer the stew until the rabbit is tender — about 35 minutes.

Meanwhile, place the potatoes in a saucepan, cover them with cold water, and bring the water to a boil. Reduce the heat to maintain a strong simmer; cook the potatoes until they are tender — about five minutes.

Bring 4 cups of water to a boil in another saucepan. Add the corn and cook for five minutes. Remove the rounds with a slotted spoon and set them aside. If you are using fresh lima beans, blanch them in the same boiling water for eight to 10 minutes, then drain them. (If you are using frozen limas, do not blanch them.)

When the rabbit finishes cooking, add the fresh blanched or frozen lima beans and the remaining ¼ teaspoon of salt to the pot; reduce the heat to low and cook the stew for two to three minutes more. Divide the potatoes and corn among four individual bowls and ladle the stew over the top.

Duck Stew with Watercress

Serves 4
Working time: about one hour and 50 minutes
Total time: about 3 hours

Calories **485**
Protein **31g.**
Cholesterol **109mg.**
Total fat **20g.**
Saturated fat **7g.**
Sodium **430mg.**

1 tbsp. safflower oil
one 4-lb. duck, skinned (technique, page 55) and quartered, all visible fat removed, the neck and back reserved
2 cups dry white wine
2 cups unsalted brown, veal or chicken stock
3 onions, 1 peeled and studded with 6 cloves, the other 2 finely chopped
1 carrot, quartered lengthwise and cut into ¾-inch pieces
1½ lb. ripe tomatoes, peeled, seeded and coarsely chopped, or 14 oz. canned unsalted tomatoes, seeded and coarsely chopped
½ tsp. salt
freshly ground black pepper
1 tbsp. unsalted butter
4 garlic cloves, chopped
1½ tsp. fresh rosemary, or ½ tsp. dried rosemary
3 tbsp. flour
1 bunch watercress, stemmed

Heat the oil in a large, heavy-bottomed skillet over medium-high heat. Add the duck quarters, neck and back, and sauté them until they are well browned on one side — about eight minutes. Turn the pieces over and sauté them on the second side for about seven minutes. Then transfer the duck pieces to a large, heavy-bottomed pot.

Pour off and discard the fat in the skillet. Add the wine to the skillet and bring it to a boil, using a wooden spoon to scrape up the caramelized bits from the bottom of the skillet. Boil the wine until it is reduced to about 1 cup — five to 10 minutes.

Add the reduced wine to the pot along with the stock, 4 cups of water and the clove-studded onion. Slowly bring the stew to a boil over medium heat. Skim off any impurities that rise to the surface; pour in ½ cup of cold water and skim again. Bring the stew to a boil again, reduce the heat to maintain a simmer and skim once more. Simmer the stew for 35 minutes, turning the duck pieces once.

Add the carrot, tomatoes, ¼ teaspoon of the salt and some pepper. Simmer the stew until the duck pieces are tender — about 30 minutes more. Remove the duck pieces from the pot and set them aside; discard the neck and back. Reduce the stew liquid over high heat to about 3 cups — five to 10 minutes.

While the stew liquid is reducing, melt the butter in a saucepan over medium heat. Add the finely chopped onions, garlic, rosemary and the remaining ¼ teaspoon of salt; cook, stirring from time to time, for 10 minutes. Add ½ cup of the reduced stew liquid to the pan and continue cooking until the onions are very limp — about 10 minutes more.

Stir the flour into the pan, then whisk in another cup of the reduced stew liquid. Simmer the mixture for one minute, then transfer it to a blender or food processor and purée it, stopping once to scrape down the sides. Whisk the purée into the stew liquid.

With a sharp knife, remove the duck meat from the bones. Discard the bones and cut the meat into ½-inch pieces. Add the duck pieces to the stew liquid. Grind in some more pepper. Reheat the mixture over low heat for five minutes, then stir in the watercress and immediately remove the pot from the heat. Serve the stew with egg noodles.

Lamb-Spinach Stew with Orzo

Serves 4
Working time: about 15 minutes
Total time: about 1 hour and 15 minutes

Calories **485**
Protein **29g.**
Cholesterol **54mg.**
Total fat **19g.**
Saturated fat **9g.**
Sodium **425mg.**

1 tbsp. safflower oil
1 onion, chopped
6 garlic cloves, finely chopped
1 tsp. ground cumin
1 tsp. ground coriander
1 lb. boneless lamb, cut into 1-inch chunks
½ tsp. salt
freshly ground black pepper
3 cups unsalted brown stock
1 cup orzo
1 lb. spinach, washed and stemmed
juice of ½ lime

Heat the oil in a large, heavy-bottomed pot over medium-high heat. Add the onion, garlic, cumin and coriander, and sauté the mixture until the onion is translucent — about four minutes. Add the lamb and cook it until it loses all trace of redness — about three minutes. Add the salt and a generous grinding of pepper. Then pour in the stock, reduce the heat, and simmer the liquid, covered, until the lamb is tender — about one hour.

In a large pot, about 15 minutes before the lamb is done, add the orzo to 12 cups of boiling water with 1½ teaspoons of salt. Start testing the orzo after 10 minutes and cook it until it is *al dente*. Drain the orzo and rinse it under cold running water.

When the lamb is done, degrease the liquid *(box, page 55)*. Then add the spinach to the pot and tightly cover it. Cook the spinach until it is wilted — about three minutes. Stir in the cooked orzo and the lime juice just before serving the stew.

Veal Stew with Pearl Onions and Grainy Mustard

Serves 6
Working time: about 15 minutes
Total time: about 1 hour

Calories **270**
Protein **23g.**
Cholesterol **80mg.**
Total fat **13g.**
Saturated fat **7g.**
Sodium **135mg.**

1½ lb. veal stew meat, trimmed and cut into 1-inch cubes
2 cups unsalted veal or chicken stock
½ cup dry white wine
2 small onions, peeled, each stuck with 2 cloves
1 tsp. fresh thyme, or ¼ tsp. dried thyme leaves
1½ tbsp. unsalted butter
¼ cup flour
1 large carrot, cut diagonally into ¼-inch-thick slices
8 oz. pearl onions, peeled
1 tbsp. grainy mustard
¼ cup light cream
⅛ tsp. white pepper

Combine the veal, stock, wine, the clove-studded onions and 2 cups of water in a large pot. Bring the liquid to a boil and skim off any impurities that rise to the surface. Add the thyme, then reduce the heat. Simmer the meat, partially covered, until it is just tender — about 40 minutes. Remove and discard the onions.

Melt the butter in a small saucepan over medium heat. Whisk in the flour and cook the mixture, whisking constantly, for three minutes. Continuing to whisk, slowly pour in 2 cups of the veal-cooking liquid until a smooth mixture results. Transfer this liquid to the pot and bring the stew to a boil. Reduce the heat, add the carrot and pearl onions, and stir in the mustard. Simmer the stew until the vegetables are tender — about 10 minutes. Gently stir in the cream and pepper; serve the stew immediately.

Mexican Chicken Stew with Ancho Chilies

THIS STEW IS BEST SERVED OVER RICE. IF YOU LIKE, SCATTER HULLED TOASTED PUMPKIN SEEDS ON TOP.

Serves 4
Cooking time: about 25 minutes
Total time: about 45 minutes

Calories **260**
Protein **30g.**
Cholesterol **74mg.**
Total fat **11g.**
Saturated fat **2g.**
Sodium **680mg.**

4 cups unsalted chicken stock
2 dried ancho chili peppers, stemmed, seeded, rinsed and quartered
4 boneless chicken breast halves, skinned and cut into 1-inch cubes (about 1 lb.)
1 tsp. salt
¼ tsp. freshly ground black pepper
1½ tbsp. corn or safflower oil
1 tbsp. finely chopped garlic
½ tsp. ground cumin
⅛ tsp. ground cloves
12 oz. chayote squash or young zucchini, cut into ½-inch chunks
1 onion, coarsely chopped
2 tsp. cornstarch, mixed with 2 tbsp. water
⅔ cup chopped cilantro

Bring one cup of the stock to a boil in a small saucepan. Add the chilies, then reduce the heat, cover the pan, and simmer the liquid for five minutes. Turn off the heat and let the mixture stand for five minutes. Purée the chilies in a blender or food processor with ¼ cup of the liquid. Blend in the remaining liquid and then set the purée aside.

Toss the chicken cubes with the salt and pepper. Heat 1 tablespoon of the corn or safflower oil in a large, heavy-bottomed skillet over medium-high heat. Add the chicken cubes and sauté them, stirring frequently, until the cubes are browned — about two minutes. Remove the cubes and set them aside.

Reduce the heat under the skillet to low; add the remaining ½ tablespoon of oil, the garlic, cumin and cloves. Cook, stirring constantly, until the garlic has softened — about three minutes. Add the chili purée and the remaining three cups of stock.

Bring the liquid to a boil, then add the squash and onion. Reduce the heat, cover the skillet and simmer the mixture for 10 minutes. Remove the lid and increase the heat to medium; add the reserved chicken cubes, then stir in the cornstarch mixture. Simmer the stew until it thickens slightly and is shiny — three to four minutes. Stir in the cilantro just before serving.

Pork and Apple Stew

Serves 4
Working time: about 30 minutes
Total time: about 1 hour and 45 minutes

Calories **280**
Protein **24g.**
Cholesterol **72mg.**
Total fat **12g.**
Saturated fat **2g.**
Sodium **265mg.**

2 tbsp. safflower oil
1 lb. boneless pork shoulder, fat trimmed away, the meat cut into 1-inch chunks
1 onion, sliced
3 tart apples, 2 cut into large chunks, 1 cored and thinly sliced
1 tsp. dried sage
¼ tsp. salt
freshly ground black pepper
3 cups unsalted brown stock
1 ripe tomato, peeled, seeded and chopped

Heat 1 tablespoon of the oil in a heavy-bottomed pot over medium-high heat. Add the pork and onion, and sauté them until the pork is lightly browned and the onion is translucent — about five minutes. Add the ap-

ple chunks, sage, salt, a generous grinding of pepper and the stock. Reduce the heat to maintain a simmer, then cover the pot and cook the stew until the pork is tender — about one hour.

Remove the pork from the pot and set it aside. Carefully skim as much fat from the surface of the liquid as you can. Purée the apple chunks and onion with their cooking liquid in several batches in a food mill. (Alternatively, purée the mixture in a food processor, then press the purée through a fine sieve with a wooden spoon.) Return the purée and the pork to the pot, and heat the stew over medium-high heat.

While the stew is heating, pour the remaining tablespoon of safflower oil into a heavy-bottomed skillet over medium-high heat. Add the uncooked apple slices and sauté them until they are lightly browned. Stir the apple slices and the chopped tomato into the hot stew and serve the dish at once.

EDITOR'S NOTE: *This stew may be prepared up to 24 hours in advance, but the apple slices must be sautéed and added just before serving.*

Oxtails Braised with Carrots

Serves 4
Working time: about 35 minutes
Total time: about 3 hours

Calories **295**
Protein **32g.**
Cholesterol **75mg.**
Total fat **9g.**
Saturated fat **3g.**
Sodium **245mg.**

1 tbsp. safflower oil
1 bunch scallions, trimmed and chopped (about 1 cup)
1½ tbsp. finely chopped fresh ginger
2 garlic cloves, finely chopped
2 cups unsalted brown stock
1 cup dry sherry
2 tsp. fermented black beans, crushed
1 tsp. chili sauce
2 tsp. hoisin sauce
3 lb. oxtails, trimmed of all fat and blanched in boiling water for 3 minutes
5 carrots, roll-cut (technique, page 112)
6 oz. fresh Asian wheat noodles

In a heavy-bottomed pot large enough to hold the oxtails in a single layer, heat the oil over medium-high heat. Add the scallions, ginger and garlic, and sauté them for two minutes. Pour in the stock, 2 cups of water and the sherry, then stir in the crushed black beans, chili sauce and hoisin sauce. Add the oxtails. Bring the liquid to a boil, then reduce the heat to very low and cook the oxtails, covered, for one hour. Turn the oxtails over and cook them until they are very tender — about one and a half hours more.

Add the carrots and simmer them until they are just tender — 15 to 20 minutes.

Pour the stew into a colander set over a large bowl. Remove the oxtail meat from the bones and return it to the pot along with the carrots and other solids. Degrease the liquid *(box, page 55)*, then pour it back into the pot. Reheat the stew over medium heat. ▶

Add the noodles to 8 cups of boiling water with 1 teaspoon of salt. Start testing the noodles after three minutes and cook them until they are *al dente*. Drain the noodles, then divide them among six soup bowls. Top the noodles with the oxtails and carrots, ladle some liquid over all and serve immediately.

A Cut above the Rest

ROLL-CUTTING A CARROT. Peel a carrot or other cylindrical vegetable. With a chef's knife, cut off the tip at an oblique angle. Roll the vegetable one quarter or one third of a turn; holding the knife at the same angle, cut off another piece — it will have non-parallel ends. Continue until you reach the stem end.

Sauerbraten Stew with Candied Ginger

Serves 4
Working time: about 30 minutes
Total time: about 3 hours (includes marinating)

Calories **345**
Protein **27g.**
Cholesterol **75mg.**
Total fat **10g.**
Saturated fat **3g.**
Sodium **390mg.**

1 tbsp. safflower oil
1 lb. lean stew beef, trimmed of fat, sliced ¼ inch thick and cut into 1-inch squares
¼ cup crystallized ginger, cut into thin strips
1 onion, finely chopped
1 carrot, finely chopped
1 celery stalk, finely chopped
1 bay leaf, crumbled
5 juniper berries, or 1 tbsp. gin
¾ tsp. ground allspice
½ tsp. salt
freshly ground black pepper
2 cups red wine
1 tbsp. red wine vinegar
1 cup unsalted brown stock
1 wheat-bread slice, crumbled
2 tsp. flour

Heat the oil in a large, heavy-bottomed skillet over medium-high heat. Add the beef and ginger, and cook them, turning the meat occasionally, until the beef is well browned — about 10 minutes. Transfer the beef and ginger to a large, nonreactive pot or casserole.

Reduce the heat under the skillet to medium, then add the onion, carrot, celery, bay leaf, juniper berries or gin, allspice, salt and some pepper. Cook the mixture, stirring and scraping with a wooden spoon to loosen any bits of beef, for five minutes. Pour in the wine and vinegar, and simmer the mixture for one minute. Transfer the vegetable mixture to the pot. Stir to combine the ingredients, then cover the pot and let the stew stand for one hour off the heat to marinate the beef and vegetables in the liquid.

Pour the stock and ¾ cup of water into the pot. Partially cover the pot and slowly bring the liquid to a simmer. Simmer the stew, stirring occasionally, for 40 minutes. Mix the crumbled bread with the flour and stir them into the stew. Continue cooking the stew until the beef is tender — about 40 minutes more.

EDITOR'S NOTE: *Crystallized ginger is simply young ginger that has been preserved in sugar.*

Beef Stew with Stout

Serves 6
Working time: about 40 minutes
Total time: about 2 hours and 15 minutes

Calories **260**
Protein **27g.**
Cholesterol **75mg.**
Total fat **10g.**
Saturated fat **3g.**
Sodium **265mg.**

1½ tbsp. safflower oil
1½ lb. lean stew beef, trimmed and cut into 1-inch cubes
1 large onion, chopped
8 oz. button mushrooms, wiped clean and halved
2 tbsp. dark brown sugar
2 cups unsalted brown or veal stock
12 oz. stout or dark beer
½ tsp. salt
freshly ground black pepper

Heat 1 tablespoon of the safflower oil in a large, heavy-bottomed skillet over medium-high heat. Add the beef cubes and sauté them, turning them frequently, until they are browned all over — about eight minutes. Using a slotted spoon, transfer the beef to a heavy-bottomed pot.

Add the remaining ½ tablespoon of oil to the skillet along with the onion, mushrooms and brown sugar. Sauté the mixture, stirring frequently, until the mushrooms begin to brown and their liquid has evaporated — about 10 minutes. Transfer the onion-mushroom mixture to the pot, then add the stock, the stout or dark beer, the salt and some pepper.

Reduce the heat to very low, cover the pot, and gently simmer the stew until the beef is tender — one and a half to two hours.

Chicken Stew in Whole Green and Red Peppers

Serves 4
Working time: about 25 minutes
Total time: about 50 minutes

Calories **200**
Protein **16g.**
Cholesterol **46mg.**
Total fat **11g.**
Saturated fat **2g.**
Sodium **330mg.**

1½ tbsp. virgin olive oil
2 large garlic cloves, finely chopped
1 onion, cut in half, the halves cut into pieces about 1 inch square
4 chicken thighs, skinned and boned, the meat cut into 1-inch chunks
1 tbsp. dried oregano
freshly ground black pepper
½ tsp. salt
1½ lb. ripe tomatoes, peeled, seeded and coarsely chopped, with their juice, or 14 oz. canned unsalted whole tomatoes, with their juice
3 green peppers, 1 seeded, deribbed and cut into 1-inch squares
3 sweet red peppers, 1 seeded, deribbed and cut into 1-inch squares

Pour the oil into a large, heavy-bottomed skillet over medium-high heat. When the oil is hot, add the garlic and onion and sauté them, stirring often, for two minutes. Add the chicken, oregano, pepper and salt, and sauté the chicken until the pieces are golden brown — about five minutes.

Reduce the heat and add the tomatoes with their juice to the skillet; if you are using canned whole tomatoes, coarsely chop the tomatoes in the skillet. Then add the squares of green and red pepper. Cover the skillet and simmer the stew until the chicken is tender and the peppers are soft — about 20 minutes. If the stew absorbs all the liquid, pour in ½ cup of water.

While the stew is simmering, carefully cut the top off each of the remaining peppers. Seed and derib the peppers. If necessary, shave a thin slice from the bottom of each pepper so it will stand upright. Set a steamer in a saucepan and pour in enough water to barely reach the bottom of the steamer. Bring the water to a boil, put the peppers in the steamer and tightly cover the pan. Steam the peppers until they are tender — five to 10 minutes.

Stand each steamed pepper in a small bowl. Spoon the stew into the peppers; distribute any remaining stew around the peppers and serve immediately.

Beef Stew with Apricots and Couscous

Serves 4
Working time: about 10 minutes
Total time: about 1 hour and 15 minutes

Calories **475**
Protein **34g.**
Cholesterol **76mg.**
Total fat **10g.**
Saturated fat **3g.**
Sodium **450mg.**

½ tsp. salt
freshly ground black pepper
1 lb. lean beef-stew meat, cut into 1-inch cubes
2 tbsp. flour
1 tbsp. safflower oil
1 small onion, thinly sliced
1 garlic clove, finely chopped
½ cup dry vermouth
½ tsp. ground cinnamon
6 oz. dried apricots, cut in half if large
3 cups unsalted brown stock
1 lb. peas, shelled (about 1 cup), or 1 cup frozen peas, defrosted
1 cup couscous

Sprinkle ¼ teaspoon of the salt and some pepper over the beef cubes, then dredge them in the flour.

Heat the oil in a large, nonreactive, heavy-bottomed casserole over medium-high heat. Add the beef cubes and sauté them, turning them frequently, until they are browned on all sides — about three minutes. Push the beef to one side of the skillet; reduce the heat to medium, add the onion and garlic, and cook them, stirring often, until the onion is translucent — about four minutes. Stir in the vermouth and cinnamon. Scrape the bottom of the pan with a wooden spoon to dissolve the caramelized juices and bits of flour. Simmer the liquid until it thickens — two to three minutes.

Stir in one third of the apricots and half of the stock. Bring the liquid to a gentle simmer over medium-low heat and cook it, covered, for 30 minutes. Stir in the remaining 1½ cups of stock and cook the mixture, covered, for 20 minutes more. Add the remaining apricots along with the fresh peas, if you are using them (do not add the frozen peas yet). Cook the stew for an additional 10 minutes; if you are using frozen peas, stir them in about three minutes before the end of the cooking time.

To prepare the couscous, bring 1½ cups of water to a boil in a small saucepan with the remaining ¼ teaspoon of salt. Remove the pan from the heat, stir in the couscous and let it stand, covered, for five minutes. Fluff the couscous with a fork and serve it blanketed with the stew.

Seafood Stew with Water Chestnuts

Serves 4
Working time: about 35 minutes
Total time: about 50 minutes

Calories **240**
Protein **25g.**
Cholesterol **101mg.**
Total fat **6g.**
Saturated fat **1g.**
Sodium **165mg.**

12 oz. black-sea-bass fillets (or grouper or red snapper)
1½ tbsp. finely chopped fresh ginger
1 garlic clove, finely chopped
¼ cup mirin (sweetened Japanese rice wine) or cream sherry
¼ tsp. freshly ground black pepper
8 oz. large shrimp, peeled, deveined if necessary
1 tbsp. peanut oil
1 cup fish stock
1 tsp. dark soy sauce
2 carrots, thinly sliced diagonally
4 scallions, trimmed and thinly sliced diagonally
8 fresh water chestnuts, peeled and thinly sliced, or 8 canned water chestnuts, drained, rinsed and thinly sliced
4 oz. mushrooms, wiped clean and thinly sliced (about 1 cup)
4 tsp. cornstarch, mixed with 2 tbsp. water
1 bunch watercress, stemmed

Rinse the fish under cold running water, then pat it dry with paper towels and slice it into 1-inch cubes.

In a bowl, combine the ginger, garlic, mirin or sherry, and pepper. Add the fish and shrimp, stir to coat them with the marinade, and let the mixture stand at room temperature for 20 minutes.

Drain and reserve the marinade. Heat the oil in a large casserole over medium-high heat. Add the fish and shrimp, and stir fry them until they are opaque — two to three minutes. Remove the seafood from the casserole and set it aside while you finish the dish.

Pour the stock, soy sauce and reserved marinade into the casserole. Add the carrots, scallions, water chestnuts and mushrooms. Bring the stew to a boil, then reduce the heat to maintain a gentle simmer, and cover the casserole. Cook the stew until the carrots are tender — about eight minutes.

Stir in the cornstarch mixture, watercress and reserved seafood. Return the stew to a boil and cook it for two minutes more to thicken it. Serve immediately.

Southwest Gumbo

Serves 8
Working time: about 40 minutes
Total time: about 1 hour

Calories **290**
Protein **32g.**
Cholesterol **109mg.**
Total fat **8g.**
Saturated fat **1g.**
Sodium **390mg.**

3 tbsp. olive oil
8 oz. fresh okra, trimmed and cut into 1-inch lengths
1 large onion, coarsely chopped
1 cup very finely chopped celery
1 large garlic clove, finely chopped
1 large shallot, finely chopped
3 tbsp. masa harina
1 tsp. filé powder
1 tsp. salt
1 tsp. sugar
1 tsp. freshly ground black pepper
1 tsp. ground cumin
4 cups fish stock
1 green pepper, seeded, deribbed and coarsely chopped
1 sweet red pepper, seeded, deribbed and coarsely chopped
1 lb. tomatillos, husked, cored and cut into thin wedges
⅓ cup chopped fresh parsley
2 tbsp. finely chopped cilantro
8 drops hot red-pepper sauce
1 lb. halibut steaks (or sea bass), rinsed, skinned and cut into 1-inch cubes
1 lb. orange roughy fillets (or grouper), rinsed and cut into 1-inch pieces
1 lb. medium shrimp, peeled, deveined if necessary

Heat 1 tablespoon of the olive oil in a large, heavy-bottomed, nonreactive pot over medium-high heat. Add the okra and sauté it, turning frequently, until it is evenly browned — about five minutes. Remove the okra and set it aside.

Reduce the heat to medium and pour the remaining 2 tablespoons of oil into the pot. Add the onion and celery and cook them, covered, until the onion is translucent — about five minutes. Add the garlic and shallot and cook the mixture, stirring constantly, for two minutes more. Sprinkle in the masa harina, filé powder, salt, sugar, black pepper and cumin. Whisk in the stock and bring the liquid to a boil. Add the okra, the green pepper and red pepper, and the tomatillos. Partially cover the pot, then reduce the heat to maintain a simmer and cook the gumbo, stirring occasionally, for eight to 10 minutes.

Stir in the parsley, cilantro and red-pepper sauce. Add the halibut, orange roughy and shrimp, and gently stir the gumbo to incorporate the fish and shrimp. Cover the pot, reduce the heat to low and cook the gumbo for five minutes more. Serve immediately.

EDITOR'S NOTE: *Masa harina — finely ground white or yellow hominy — may be obtained at large supermarkets. If it is unavailable, substitute flour. Filé powder, used to flavor and thicken Creole soups and stews, is made from dried young sassafras leaves.*

Cod Stewed with Onions, Potatoes, Corn and Tomatoes

Serves 6
Working time: about 15 minutes
Total time: about 1 hour

Calories **310**
Protein **19g.**
Cholesterol **32mg.**
Total fat **4g.**
Saturated fat **1g.**
Sodium **305mg.**

1 tbsp. virgin olive oil
3 onions (about 1 lb.), thinly sliced
5 boiling potatoes (about 2 lb.), peeled and thinly sliced
2 cups fresh or frozen corn kernels
½ green pepper, seeded, deribbed and diced
hot red-pepper sauce
1 lb. cod (or haddock or pollock), skinned, rinsed under cold running water, and cut into chunks
2½ lb. ripe tomatoes, peeled, seeded and chopped, or 28 oz. canned unsalted whole tomatoes, drained and chopped
¼ tsp. salt
freshly ground black pepper
cilantro leaves for garnish (optional)

In a large, heavy-bottomed pot, heat the oil over medium heat. Add a layer of onions and a layer of potatoes. Sprinkle some of the corn and green pepper on top. Dribble a few drops of red-pepper sauce over the vegetables. Add a layer of fish and tomatoes and season with a little of the salt and some pepper. Repeat the process, building up successive layers, until the remaining vegetables and fish are used. Cover the pot and cook over medium-low heat until the potatoes are done — about 45 minutes. Garnish the stew with the cilantro leaves if you are using them. Serve at once.

Mediterranean Fish Chowder

Serves 6
Working time: about 40 minutes
Total time: about 1 hour and 30 minutes

Calories **235**
Protein **23g.**
Cholesterol **121mg.**
Total fat **3g.**
Saturated fat **1g.**
Sodium **315mg.**

8 oz. shrimp, peeled, deveined if necessary, the shells reserved
2 leeks, trimmed, split and washed thoroughly to remove all grit, green and white parts sliced separately
12 black peppercorns
1 tsp. chopped fresh thyme, or ¼ tsp. dried thyme leaves
1 tsp. chopped fresh rosemary, or ¼ tsp. dried rosemary
1 bay leaf
2 lb. mussels, scrubbed and debearded
8 oz. crab meat, picked over
1 garlic clove, finely chopped
pinch of saffron
¼ cup dry white wine
1 lb. boiling potatoes, peeled and cut into 1-inch chunks
1½ lb. ripe tomatoes, peeled, seeded and chopped, or 14 oz. canned unsalted tomatoes, drained and crushed

Pour 4 cups of water into a large pot. Add the shrimp shells, green leek parts, peppercorns, thyme, rose-mary and bay leaf. Bring the broth to a boil, then reduce the heat and simmer the liquid for 15 minutes. Add the mussels to the broth and cook them until they open — about three minutes. Transfer the opened mussels to a bowl. Cook the remaining mussels for two minutes more and transfer the opened ones to the bowl; discard any that remain closed.

Working over the bowl to catch their juices, free the mussels from their shells and drop them into the bowl. Add the shrimp, crab meat, garlic, saffron and wine, and stir well. Let the shellfish marinate at room temperature for 30 minutes.

In the meantime, strain the broth through a fine sieve, discarding the solids. Return the broth to the pot over medium-high heat. Add the white leek parts and the potatoes, and cook them until the leeks are tender — about 15 minutes. Stir in the tomatoes and cook the stew until the potatoes are tender — about five minutes more.

Add the shellfish and its marinade to the stew. Cook the stew until the shrimp are opaque and the other shellfish are warmed through — about three minutes. Serve immediately.

Smoked and Fresh Salmon in Red Wine Stew

Serves 8
Working time: about 45 minutes
Total time: about 1 hour and 15 minutes

Calories **240**
Protein **15g.**
Cholesterol **22mg.**
Total fat **7g.**
Saturated fat **1g.**
Sodium **90mg.**

2 red potatoes, scrubbed and cut into ½-inch chunks
1 tbsp. safflower oil
8 oz. mushrooms, wiped clean and sliced
10 oz. pearl onions, blanched in boiling water for 30 seconds and peeled
½ tsp. sugar
3 cups fish stock or unsalted chicken stock
3 cups red wine
½ tsp. fresh thyme, or ⅛ tsp. dried thyme leaves
1 bay leaf
1 tbsp. cornstarch, mixed with 2 tbsp. water
2 oz. smoked salmon, cut into ¼-inch squares
1 lb. salmon fillet, skinned, rinsed and cut into 1-inch-square pieces

Put the potato cubes into a saucepan and pour in enough water to cover them by about 2 inches. Bring the water to a boil, then reduce the heat and simmer the potatoes until they are tender — about 10 minutes. Drain the potatoes and set them aside.

While the potatoes are cooking, heat the oil in a large, nonreactive heavy-bottomed pot over medium-high heat. Add the mushrooms and cook them, stirring frequently, until they are browned and the liquid has evaporated — about five minutes. Remove the mushrooms from the pot and set them aside.

Add the onions, sugar and 1 cup of the stock to the pot. Cook, stirring frequently and scraping the bottom of the pot, until almost all the liquid has evaporated and the onions begin to caramelize — about 10 minutes. Then remove the onions and set them aside with the mushrooms.

Pour the wine and the remaining 2 cups of stock into the pot. Add the thyme and bay leaf. Bring the liquid to a boil, stirring constantly and scraping the bottom of the pot to dissolve the caramelized juices. Lower the heat, then partially cover the pot and simmer the liquid until it is reduced to approximately 4 cups — about 30 minutes.

Add the potatoes, mushrooms, onions and the cornstarch mixture to the liquid and bring it to a boil. Reduce the heat, stir in the smoked salmon and fresh salmon, and simmer the stew until the salmon is opaque — two to three minutes. Serve hot.

Squid and Red-Bean Stew

Serves 6
Working (and total) time: about 1 hour and 45 minutes

Calories **275**	1 cup dried red or kidney beans, picked over
Protein **23g.**	1 tbsp. safflower oil
Cholesterol **208mg.**	1 small onion, thinly sliced
Total fat **4g.**	1 garlic clove, finely chopped
Saturated fat **0g.**	½ cup Marsala
Sodium **265mg.**	8 oz. mushrooms, wiped clean, the large ones quartered, the smaller ones halved
	1½ lb. ripe tomatoes, peeled, seeded and finely chopped, or 14 oz. canned unsalted tomatoes, chopped, with their juice
	¾ lb. squid, cleaned
	6 oz. green beans, trimmed and cut into 2-inch lengths
	1 tsp. fresh oregano, or ¼ tsp. dried oregano
	½ tsp. salt
	freshly ground black pepper

Rinse the beans under cold running water, then transfer them to a large, heavy-bottomed pot and pour in enough cold water to cover the beans by about 3 inches. Discard any beans that float to the surface. Cover the pot, leaving the lid ajar, and slowly bring the liquid to a boil over medium-low heat. Boil the beans for two minutes, then turn off the heat and soak the beans, covered, for at least one hour. (Alternatively, soak the beans overnight in cold water.)

Pour the oil into a large pot over medium heat. Add the onion and cook it, stirring often, until it is translucent — about four minutes. Add the garlic and cook it, stirring, for one minute. Pour in the Marsala and continue cooking until the liquid is reduced by half — three to four minutes.

Stir in the mushrooms, tomatoes, soaked beans and 5 cups of water. Increase the heat to high and bring the liquid to a boil. Immediately reduce the heat to maintain a simmer; cook the mixture, covered, for 30 minutes.

While the liquid is simmering, prepare the squid. Cut the squid into strips about 2 inches long and ¼ inch wide. Cut the tentacles into 2-inch lengths. Add the squid to the stew and continue simmering the stew until the beans are tender — about one hour more.

While the stew is cooking, bring 4 cups of water to a boil in a saucepan. Add the green beans and cook them until they are barely tender — about eight minutes. Drain the green beans and set them aside.

When the beans in the stew are tender, add the green beans to the pot along with the oregano, salt and some pepper. Simmer the stew over low heat until the green beans are heated through — three to four minutes. Serve the stew piping hot.

Caribbean Red-Snapper Stew

Serves 4
Working time: about 15 minutes
Total time: about 45 minutes

Calories **265**	1 lb. red snapper fillets (or Pacific rockfish), skin left on
Protein **25g.**	¼ cup dry white wine
Cholesterol **46mg.**	2 tbsp. dark rum
Total fat **5g.**	1 tbsp. finely chopped fresh ginger
Saturated fat **1g.**	1 garlic clove, finely chopped
Sodium **250mg.**	freshly ground black pepper
	1 tbsp. safflower oil
	1 onion, cut into small chunks
	2 tbsp. flour
	2 tsp. tomato paste
	1 green pepper, seeded, deribbed and cut into ¾-inch pieces
	2 cups fish stock
	2 ripe tomatoes, peeled, seeded and coarsely chopped
	1 ripe mango, peeled and cut into ¾-inch pieces
	¼ tsp. salt

Rinse the fillets under cold running water and pat them dry with paper towels. Cut the fillets into 1½-inch squares and set them aside.

In a bowl, combine the wine, rum, ginger, garlic and some pepper. Marinate the fish pieces in this mixture for 30 minutes in the refrigerator.

When the fish has marinated for 20 minutes, pour the oil into a nonreactive, heavy-bottomed pot over medium heat. Add the onion chunks and cook them, stirring occasionally, until they begin to brown — six to eight minutes. Stir in the flour, then the tomato paste and the green pepper. Slowly whisk in the stock. Drain the marinade from the fish and add it to the pot. Bring the liquid to a simmer and cook it for three minutes.

Add the fish, tomatoes, mango and salt to the pot. Cover the pot and simmer the stew until the fish is opaque and flakes easily — about seven minutes. Serve immediately.

Shrimp Creole

Serves 4
Working time: about 35 minutes
Total time: about 1 hour and 15 minutes

Calories **325**
Protein **23g.**
Cholesterol **163mg.**
Total fat **6g.**
Saturated fat **1g.**
Sodium **240mg.**

4 tsp. safflower oil
1 large onion, thinly sliced
2 garlic cloves, finely chopped
1 tbsp. flour
1 tbsp. chili powder
1¼ lb. large shrimp, peeled, deveined if necessary, the shells reserved
1 cup vermouth
½ cup rice
3 Italian or other mild green peppers, seeded, deribbed and cut lengthwise into thin strips
1 celery stalk, thinly sliced on the diagonal
1½ lb. ripe tomatoes, peeled, seeded and coarsely chopped, with their juice, or 14 oz. canned unsalted tomatoes, chopped, with their juice
¼ tsp. filé powder (optional)
¼ tsp. salt
1 oz. lean ham (optional), julienned

Heat 2 teaspoons of the oil in a heavy-bottomed pot over medium heat. Add the onion slices and cook them, stirring frequently, until they are browned — eight to 10 minutes. Remove half of the slices and set them aside.

Add the garlic and cook it for one minute. Stir in the flour and chili powder, then the shrimp shells, vermouth and 1 cup of water. Bring the liquid to a simmer; reduce the heat to medium low, cover the pot and cook the mixture for 20 minutes to make a flavorful base for the stew.

Meanwhile, bring 1 cup of water to a boil in a small saucepan. Add the rice, stir once and reduce the heat to maintain a simmer; cook the rice, covered, until the liquid is absorbed — about 20 minutes. Set the rice aside while you finish the stew.

Heat the remaining 2 teaspoons of oil in a large, heavy-bottomed skillet over medium-high heat. Add the shrimp to the skillet and sauté them, stirring, for two minutes. Stir in the peppers and celery and cook them for one minute. Add the tomatoes, the reserved onion slices and the filé powder if you are using it. Strain the stew base into the skillet and add the rice. Gently simmer the stew for five minutes. Stir in the salt and garnish the stew with the ham, if you are using it, just before serving.

EDITOR'S NOTE: *Filé powder, used to flavor and thicken Creole soups and stews, is made from dried young sassafras leaves.*

Flounder Curry

Serves 4
Working time: about 30 minutes
Total time: about 40 minutes

Calories **280**
Protein **25g.**
Cholesterol **56mg.**
Total fat **7g.**
Saturated fat **1g.**
Sodium **205mg.**

1 tbsp. chopped fresh ginger
½ tsp. turmeric
¼ tsp. ground cumin
¼ tsp. ground coriander
⅛ tsp. ground cardamom
⅛ tsp. fennel seeds
⅛ tsp. ground mace
1 tbsp. safflower oil
2 onions, sliced
1½ lb. ripe tomatoes, peeled, seeded and chopped, or 14 oz. canned unsalted tomatoes, drained and crushed
2 cups fish stock or unsalted chicken stock
1 lb. mushrooms, wiped clean and halved
juice of ½ lemon
1 lb. flounder fillets (or other lean, white-fleshed fish)

Put the ginger, turmeric, cumin, coriander, cardamom, fennel seeds and mace into a mortar; with a pestle, grind the seasonings to a paste. Set the paste aside.

Heat the oil in a large, nonreactive, heavy-bottomed skillet over medium-high heat. Add the onions and sauté them until they are translucent — about four minutes. Stir in the spice paste, tomatoes and stock, and bring the liquid to a boil. Add the mushrooms and lemon juice. Lower the heat and simmer the curry until it is reduced by half — eight to 12 minutes.

Meanwhile, rinse the fillets under cold running water and pat them dry with paper towels. Slice the fillets into 1-inch-wide strips. Lay the strips on top of the curry, cover the skillet, and steam the fish until it is opaque — about two minutes. Serve immediately.

Trout Stew with Zucchini, Capers and Watercress

Serves 4
Working time: about 40 minutes
Total time: about 1 hour

Calories **240**
Protein **23g.**
Cholesterol **64mg.**
Total fat **10g.**
Saturated fat **1g.**
Sodium **185mg.**

1 tbsp. safflower oil
1 onion, sliced
1 tbsp. flour
½ cup dry white wine
2 cups fish stock
1 tsp. fresh thyme, or ¼ tsp. dried thyme leaves
¼ tsp. dry mustard
12 oz. zucchini, quartered lengthwise and cut into strips about 1 ½ inches long and ¼ inch wide
1 tsp. capers, rinsed and drained
1 lb. trout fillets
¼ cup chopped watercress leaves

Heat the oil in a large, nonreactive, heavy-bottomed casserole or pot over medium-high heat. Add the onion slices and sauté them until they are translucent — about four minutes. Sprinkle in the flour and stir to coat the onions evenly. Pour in the wine and boil the liquid, stirring, until it is reduced to about 1 tablespoon — approximately three minutes. Whisk in the stock, thyme and mustard. Reduce the heat and simmer the mixture, partially covered, for 15 minutes.

Add the zucchini and capers, and continue simmering the mixture until the zucchini is tender — about five minutes. Meanwhile, rinse the fillets under cold running water and pat them dry with paper towels, then cut them into 1-inch chunks. Arrange the fish pieces on top of the vegetables and cover the casserole. Cook the stew until the fish is opaque — about three minutes. Gently stir in the watercress and serve.

Lobster Navarin

ALTHOUGH A TRADITIONAL NAVARIN FEATURES LAMB, THE
FOCAL POINT HERE IS LOBSTER, WHOSE RICH FLAVOR MAKES
FOR AN EQUALLY SUCCULENT STEW. THE TECHNIQUE OF
"TURNING" VEGETABLES IS SHOWN OVERLEAF.

Serves 2
Working (and total) time: about 1 hour and 30 minutes

Calories **325**
Protein **24g.**
Cholesterol **109mg.**
Total fat **11g.**
Saturated fat **6g.**
Sodium **390mg.**

1 live lobster (about 2 lb.)
1 tbsp. unsalted butter
1 cup chopped onion
1 tsp. flour
1 carrot, turned
1 turnip, turned
1 cucumber, turned
1 tsp. tomato paste
2 tbsp. Cognac or Armagnac
freshly ground black pepper
2 tbsp. light cream

Pour enough water into a pot to fill it about 1 inch
deep; bring the water to a boil and add the lobster.
Cover the pot and cook the lobster until it turns a
bright red-orange — about 15 minutes. Remove the
lobster from the pot and set it aside until it is cool
enough to handle. Do not discard the liquid.

Working over the pot to catch the juices, twist off
the lobster tail. Snip down either side of the undershell,
then remove the meat in one piece and set it aside. Put
the shells into the pot. Crack the claws; remove the
claw and joint meat, cut it into small pieces, and set it
aside separately from the tail. Put all of the shells into
the pan. Scoop the green tomalley out of the lobster
body and, if desired, reserve it for another use. Hold
the body under cold running water to rinse it out.
Break the body and add it to the pan with the shells.

Pour 4 cups of water into the pot and bring the
mixture to a boil. Boil the liquid for 15 minutes, then
strain it through a fine sieve into a bowl. Discard the
shells when all of their liquid has drained into the bowl.

In the pot, melt the butter over medium heat. Add
the onion and cook it until it is translucent — about five
minutes. Stir in the flour and cook for one minute
more. Pour half of the strained lobster liquid back into
the pan. Bring this mixture to a boil, stirring several
times, and continue cooking until almost all of the ▶

liquid has evaporated — about 15 minutes.

Meanwhile, transfer the liquid remaining in the bowl to a small saucepan and bring it to a boil. Add the carrot pieces and cook them for one and one half minutes. Add the turnip pieces and cook for one and one half minutes more, then add the cucumber pieces and continue cooking for another 30 seconds. Remove the vegetables with a slotted spoon and set them aside. Do not discard the liquid.

Transfer the reduced onion mixture to a blender or food processor; add the tomato paste and the liquid from the small saucepan, and purée the mixture.

Return the purée to the pot over medium-low heat. Add the claw and joint meat, the turned vegetables, the brandy and some pepper. Cook the navarin until it is heated through — about four minutes.

While the navarin heats, slice the tail into eight rounds. Divide the rounds between two serving bowls. Stir the cream into the pot, then spoon the navarin around the lobster in the bowls. Serve immediately.

Turning Vegetables to Elegant Effect

1 *CUTTING A VEGETABLE DOWN TO SIZE. To show-case vegetables, first cut them into rectangles or cylinders about 1 ½ inches long: For a turnip, as shown below, slice off the top and bottom, then cut the turnip in half. Slice each half into six to eight pieces.*

2 *TURNING THE PIECES. Holding one of the vegetable pieces between your thumb and fingertips, shave off lengthwise strips (above). Rotate the piece and repeat the cut until the piece resembles an elongated olive. Use the trimmings for soup or stock.*

Seafood Chili with Peppers and Tomatillos

Serves 4
Working time: about 1 hour and 15 minutes
Total time: about 3 hours and 30 minutes
(includes soaking)

Calories **450**
Protein **34g.**
Cholesterol **68mg.**
Total fat **14g.**
Saturated fat **1g.**
Sodium **305mg.**

1 cup black beans, picked over
8 oz. bay scallops, rinsed
4 oz. small shrimp, peeled, deveined if necessary
4 oz. tilefish fillet (or haddock or sea bass), rinsed and cut into pieces about 2 inches long and 1 inch wide
1 lime, carefully peeled to remove the white pith, sliced into thin rounds
1 ¼ tsp. ground cumin
⅛ tsp. ground ginger
1 tbsp. plus ¼ tsp. chili powder
3 tbsp. coarsely chopped cilantro
2 garlic cloves, finely chopped
½ jalapeño pepper, seeded and finely chopped (caution, page 95)
3 tbsp. safflower oil
1 onion, cut into chunks the size of the scallops
½ tsp. dried tarragon
¼ tsp. salt
¼ tsp. ground cloves
⅛ tsp. ground cinnamon
⅛ tsp. cayenne pepper
1 ½ cups unsalted chicken stock
8 oz. canned crushed tomatoes, with their juice
10 tomatillos, husked and quartered
1 sweet red pepper, seeded, deribbed and cut into chunks the size of the tomatillo quarters
1 yellow pepper, seeded, deribbed and cut into chunks the size of the tomatillo quarters

Rinse the beans under cold running water, then put them into a large pot and pour in enough cold water to cover them by about 3 inches. Discard any beans that float to the surface. Cover the pot, leaving the lid ajar, and bring the liquid to a boil over medium-low heat. Boil the beans for two minutes, then turn off the heat, cover the pot, and soak them for at least one hour. (Alternatively, soak the beans overnight in cold water.)

Drain the beans in a colander and return them to the pot. Pour in enough water to cover the beans by about 3 inches, and bring the liquid to a boil over medium-low heat. Reduce the heat to maintain a strong simmer and cover the pot. Cook the beans, stirring occasionally and skimming any foam from the surface, until they are tender — one and a half to two hours.

While the beans are cooking, combine in a large, nonreactive bowl the scallops, shrimp, fish pieces, lime, ¼ teaspoon of the cumin, the ginger, ¼ teaspoon of the chili powder, 1 tablespoon of the cilantro, half of the garlic, the jalapeño pepper and 1 tablespoon of the oil. Marinate the seafood in this mixture for 30 minutes at room temperature.

While the seafood is marinating, prepare the chili base. Heat 1 tablespoon of the remaining oil in a large, heavy-bottomed pot over medium heat. Add the onion and the remaining garlic, and cook until the onion is translucent — about five minutes. Add the remaining teaspoon of cumin, the remaining tablespoon of chili powder, the tarragon, salt, cloves, cinnamon and cayenne pepper. Cook the mixture, stirring constantly, for two to three minutes to meld the flavors.

Gradually stir in the stock and tomatoes, and bring the mixture to a boil. Reduce the heat to medium low and cover the pot, leaving the lid slightly ajar. Simmer the liquid until it is slightly thickened — 20 to 25 minutes. Drain the beans and add them to the tomato mixture. Set the chili base aside.

Pour the remaining tablespoon of oil into a large, heavy-bottomed skillet over high heat. Add the tomatillos and pepper chunks, and sauté them for two minutes. Using a slotted spoon, carefully spread the cooked vegetables over the chili base; bring the mixture to a simmer over low heat. Arrange the marinated seafood in a layer atop the chili and vegetables, then cover the pot, and steam the chili until the scallops, shrimp and fish are opaque — seven to 10 minutes. Sprinkle the remaining 2 tablespoons of cilantro over the chili and serve immediately.

EDITOR'S NOTE: *Warm corn tortillas go well with this chili.*

3 Ready in minutes, a microwave stew made with snow peas, lettuce, carrots and zucchini gleams with a sauce of lemon juice and mustard (recipe opposite).

Microwaved Soups and Stews

A microwave oven is the ideal vehicle for quick soups and stews, as the recipe for chicken ratatouille on page 138 shows. When cooked in a microwave, the dish requires only about 45 minutes to prepare, and the cooking method preserves the vibrant colors of the vegetables. The microwave oven can also be used as a shortcut for soups prepared by other methods. The acorn-squash soup on page 132 would ordinarily have taken much longer to prepare had not the squash been cooked in the microwave first. In a regular oven, the squash would bake for as long as one and a half hours; in the microwave, it is done in just 13 minutes.

Because microwaving is so quick, flavors may not mingle and meld as they do when soups and stews are cooked conventionally. But there are ways around this dilemma. The seafood stew on page 135 adopts a proven stratagem: A touch of sugar brings unity to the dish. The vegetable stew on page 131, a mélange of snow peas, zucchini, carrots and lettuce — still crisp because the cooking time is only six minutes — comes vividly to life through the addition of Dijon mustard.

The microwave offers yet another attraction — summer use. Making a soup or stew in it during the sultry days will not raise the temperature of your kitchen. And when it comes to preparing chilled soups, the microwave can be a special blessing. A perfect example is the cold apple-and-tarragon soup on page 138, in which ingredients are microwaved for just six minutes, then puréed and refrigerated. After only an hour or so, the soup is ready to be garnished with tarragon and served — a cool counterpoint to summer's heat.

Light Vegetable Stew with Snow Peas and Mustard

Serves 6 as a side dish
Working (and total) time: about 25 minutes

Calories **70**
Protein **2g.**
Cholesterol **10mg.**
Total fat **4g.**
Saturated fat **2g.**
Sodium **95mg.**

1 zucchini, halved lengthwise and cut diagonally into ¼-inch-thick slices
1 tbsp. fresh lemon juice
2 tbsp. unsalted butter, cut into pieces
2 carrots, cut diagonally into ¼-inch-thick ovals
1 shallot, finely chopped
1 tbsp. Dijon mustard
1 head romaine lettuce, cored, the leaves torn into 2-inch pieces
1 tsp. fresh thyme, or ¼ tsp. dried thyme leaves
⅛ tsp. salt
freshly ground black pepper
4 oz. snow peas, stems and strings removed, any large pods halved diagonally

Put the zucchini into a small bowl, toss it with the lemon juice, and set the bowl aside.

Put the butter into a large bowl and microwave it on high until it melts — about one minute. Stir in the carrots, shallot and mustard. Cook the mixture on high for two minutes, stirring halfway through the cooking time.

Add the lettuce, thyme, salt and some pepper; stir the vegetables to coat them with the butter. Microwave the stew on high for one minute, stirring once after 30 seconds. Stir in the zucchini and lemon juice, then the snow peas. Cook the stew on high for three minutes more, stirring once halfway through the cooking time. Stir the vegetables one last time, cover the bowl and let the stew stand for three minutes before serving it.

Gingery Acorn Squash Soup

Serves 4
Working time: about 15 minutes
Total time: about 25 minutes

Calories **95**
Protein **3g.**
Cholesterol **7mg.**
Total fat **4g.**
Saturated fat **2g.**
Sodium **185mg.**

1 ½ lb. acorn squash
2 tsp. unsalted butter
1 small onion, finely chopped
1 garlic clove, finely chopped
1 small carrot, very thinly sliced
1 ½ cups unsalted chicken stock
¼ cup low-fat milk
½ tsp. ground ginger
¼ tsp. salt
⅛ tsp. white pepper
1 tsp. toasted sesame seeds (optional)

Put the squash in a shallow 8-by-10-inch glass baking dish and microwave it on high for 30 seconds. Remove the squash from the oven; when the squash is cool enough to handle, cut off the stem, then halve the squash lengthwise. Spoon out the seeds and place the squash halves cut sides down in the dish. Cover the dish with heavy-duty plastic wrap and microwave the squash on high for seven minutes. Let the squash stand, covered, for five minutes.

Put the butter in a bowl and cover the bowl with plastic wrap or a lid; microwave the butter on high for 45 seconds. Stir the onion, garlic and carrot into the butter, then cover the bowl and microwave it on medium (50 percent power) for four minutes more. With a spoon, carefully scoop the squash flesh into the bowl; pour in the stock and cook the mixture on high, covered, for two and a half minutes. Stir the mixture and cook it on high for two and a half minutes more.

Transfer the vegetables and stock to a food processor or blender. Pour in the milk and purée the mixture, stopping occasionally to scrape down the sides. Stir in the ginger, salt and pepper. Transfer the soup to a serving bowl; garnish it with the sesame seeds if you are using them.

Sweet-and-Sour Fish Stew

Serves 4
Working (and total) time: about 50 minutes

Calories **215**
Protein **25g.**
Cholesterol **42mg.**
Total fat **1g.**
Saturated fat **0g.**
Sodium **175mg.**

2 carrots, julienned
4 scallions, trimmed and cut into ½-inch lengths
1 tbsp. finely chopped fresh ginger
¼ tsp. dark sesame oil
2 cups fish stock
1 tbsp. sugar
2 tbsp. cornstarch, mixed with 3 tbsp. water
2 tbsp. rice vinegar or white wine vinegar
1 tsp. sweet chili sauce, or ½ tsp. crushed hot red-pepper flakes mixed with 1 tsp. corn syrup and ½ tsp. vinegar
1 tsp. low-sodium soy sauce
4 dried shiitake or Chinese black mushrooms, covered with 2 cups of boiling water and soaked for 15 minutes, stemmed and cut into narrow strips
1 lb. grouper fillet (or sea bass or tilefish), rinsed and cut into 1-inch cubes
4 oz. snow peas, strings and stems removed
½ cup drained and rinsed bamboo shoots
1 oz. cellophane (bean-thread) noodles, soaked in 2 cups hot water for 10 minutes, drained and cut into 2-inch lengths

Combine the carrots, scallions, ginger and sesame oil in a 2-quart glass bowl. Cover the container with plastic wrap and microwave it on medium (50 percent power) for three minutes. Stir in the stock, sugar, cornstarch mixture, vinegar, chili sauce or pepper-flake mixture, soy sauce and mushrooms. Cover the sweet-and-sour sauce and cook it on high for three minutes.

Arrange the fish cubes in a single layer in a shallow baking dish. Distribute the snow peas, bamboo shoots and noodles on top of the fish. Pour the sweet-and-sour sauce over all, cover, and microwave on high for two minutes. Rearrange the fish, moving the less-cooked cubes from the center of the dish to the edges. Cover the stew once more and cook it on high until the fish can be easily flaked with a fork — about two minutes. Serve immediately.

Pork and Bean-Sprout Soup

Serves 4
Working time: about 30 minutes
Total time: about 1 hour

Calories **245**
Protein **30g.**
Cholesterol **73mg.**
Total fat **5g.**
Saturated fat **2g.**
Sodium **490mg.**

½ tsp. Sichuan peppercorns, or freshly ground black pepper to taste
1 lb. lean pork, julienned
¼ tsp. cayenne pepper
¼ tsp. ground ginger
2 tbsp. Chinese black vinegar or balsamic vinegar
4 cups unsalted brown stock
1 onion, thinly sliced
6 garlic cloves, thinly sliced
8 oz. bean sprouts
2½ lb. ripe tomatoes, peeled, seeded and chopped, or 28 oz. canned unsalted tomatoes, drained and crushed
¼ cup chopped fresh parsley
2 tbsp. low-sodium soy sauce

Toast the Sichuan peppercorns, if you are using them, in a heavy-bottomed skillet over medium-high heat until they smoke — about two minutes; using a mortar and pestle, grind them to a powder. Combine the pork with the ground peppercorns or black pepper, cayenne pepper, ginger and vinegar in a small bowl. Let the mixture stand at room temperature for 30 minutes.

Pour the stock into a 2-quart glass bowl. Add the onion and garlic, and cover the bowl with plastic wrap or a lid. Microwave the liquid on high for 10 minutes. Remove the bowl from the oven and stir the mixture. Cover the bowl again and cook the liquid on high for 10 minutes more.

Meanwhile, place the bean sprouts in a colander and blanch them by pouring about 8 cups of boiling water over them. Set the bean sprouts aside.

Stir the pork and its marinade into the cooked broth. Microwave the mixture on high until it barely begins to boil, then cook on high for three minutes. Add the tomatoes, parsley, soy sauce and blanched bean sprouts. Cook the soup, uncovered, for three minutes more on high. Serve immediately.

Seafood Stew in Garlic-Tomato Sauce

Serves 6
Total (and working) time: about one hour

Calories **220**
Protein **24g.**
Cholesterol **173mg.**
Total fat **5g.**
Saturated fat **1g.**
Sodium **305mg.**

2 lb. mussels, scrubbed and debearded
½ cup dry white wine
1 tsp. chopped fresh oregano, or ¼ tsp. dried oregano
freshly ground black pepper
6 oz. squid, cleaned
1 lb. shrimp, shelled, deveined if necessary
Garlic-tomato sauce
1 onion, chopped
4 garlic cloves, finely chopped
1 tsp. chopped fresh oregano, or ¼ tsp. dried oregano
⅛ tsp. cayenne pepper
juice of 1 lime
1 tsp. sugar
1 tbsp. virgin olive oil
2½ lb. ripe tomatoes, peeled, seeded and chopped, or 28 oz. canned unsalted tomatoes, drained and chopped
1 green pepper, seeded, deribbed and cut into thin strips

Place half of the mussels, along with the wine, oregano and some black pepper, in a 2-quart bowl. Cover the bowl with plastic wrap or a lid and microwave the mussels on high, rotating the dish halfway through the cooking time, until they open — about five minutes. Remove the opened mussels and set them aside; discard any that remain closed. Cook the other half of the mussels in the same way. Do not pour out the cooking liquid.

When the mussels are cool enough to handle, remove them from their shells, working over the bowl to catch their juices. Discard the shells and set the mussels aside. Strain the liquid through a sieve lined with cheesecloth into a cup; discard the solids. Wash the cooking bowl in order to make the sauce in it.

To make the garlic-tomato sauce, put the onion, garlic, oregano, cayenne pepper, lime juice, sugar and oil into the bowl. Cover it and cook the mixture on high for two minutes. Add the tomatoes and the reserved liquid from the mussels and cook, covered, on high ▶

for 10 minutes, stirring halfway through the cooking time. Reduce the heat to medium (50 percent power) and cook the sauce for 10 minutes more, stirring after five minutes.

While the sauce is cooking, prepare the squid. Slit one side of the pouch and lay it flat, skinned side down. Using a sharp knife, score the flesh diagonally in a crosshatch pattern. Then cut the pouch into 1½-inch squares and set them aside.

Add the green pepper to the sauce and continue to cook the mixture on medium (50 percent power) until the pepper is tender — about five minutes. Stir in the mussels, squid and shrimp. Cook the dish on high for an additional two minutes and serve it hot.

Chicken Stew with Mashed Potatoes

Serves 4
Working time: about 25 minutes
Total time: about 50 minutes

Calories **355**
Protein **25g.**
Cholesterol **71mg.**
Total fat **9g.**
Saturated fat **3g.**
Sodium **330mg.**

2 lb. chicken drumsticks, skinned
freshly ground black pepper
¼ tsp. paprika, preferably Hungarian
1 garlic clove, finely chopped
1 small onion, cut into ¾-inch pieces
2 small carrots, cut into ½-inch pieces
2 celery stalks, thinly sliced
1 bay leaf
¼ tsp. salt
½ tsp. fresh thyme, or ⅛ tsp. dried thyme leaves
2 tbsp. cornstarch mixed with 2 tbsp. water
Mashed potatoes
1½ lb. small boiling potatoes (about 6)
2 tsp. finely cut chives or green scallion tops
⅛ tsp. salt
⅛ tsp. white pepper
grated nutmeg
¾ cup low-fat milk, warmed

To prepare the mashed potatoes, first prick each potato several times with a fork. Arrange the potatoes around the edge of a plate. Microwave them on high for ten minutes, stopping halfway through the cooking to turn the potatoes over. Remove the potatoes from the oven and set them aside.

Sprinkle the chicken drumsticks with some pepper and the paprika. Arrange the drumsticks in a single layer in a large, shallow baking dish; the meatier portions of the drumsticks should face outward. Place the garlic, onion, and carrot and celery pieces between the drumsticks. Pour in 1½ cups of water, then add the bay leaf, salt and thyme. Cover the dish with heavy-duty plastic wrap or a lid. Microwave the chicken on high for 12 minutes, stopping after six minutes to turn the drumsticks over.

While the chicken is cooking, cut the cooled potatoes in half and spoon out the flesh into a bowl. Discard the skins. Use a food mill or a potato masher to mash the potatoes. Add the chives or green scallion tops, salt, white pepper and a small pinch of nutmeg, then whisk in the warmed milk. Transfer the mashed potatoes to a pastry bag fitted with a large star tip.

Remove the dish with the chicken from the oven. Stir the cornstarch mixture into the liquid in the dish. Using the pastry bag, pipe a decorative band of potatoes down the center of the dish. Return the dish to the oven and cook it on high for two minutes more. Serve immediately.

Broccoli Soup with Cumin and Bay Scallops

Serves 8
Working time: about 20 minutes
Total time: about 50 minutes

Calories **140**
Protein **8g.**
Cholesterol **29mg.**
Total fat **7g.**
Saturated fat **4g.**
Sodium **280mg.**

2 tbsp. unsalted butter
1 lb. broccoli, the florets cut off, the stems peeled and cut into 1-inch lengths
2 leeks, split, washed thoroughly to remove all grit, and thinly sliced
1 large boiling potato, peeled and cut into ½-inch pieces
1 garlic clove, finely chopped
2 tsp. fresh thyme, or ½ tsp. dried thyme leaves
freshly ground black pepper
¾ tsp. salt
4 cups unsalted chicken stock
¾ tsp. ground cumin
2 tbsp. fresh lemon juice
½ cup light cream
8 oz. bay scallops, the firm white connective tissue removed

Put 1 tablespoon of the butter into a 4-quart casserole. Add the broccoli, leeks, potato, garlic, thyme and some pepper. Cover the casserole with a lid or heavy-duty plastic wrap, then microwave the vegetables on high for five minutes.

Add the salt, stock, 3 cups of water and the cumin. Cover the dish, then microwave the mixture on high for 15 minutes, stirring every five minutes. Stir in the lemon juice and cook the mixture on high for 15 minutes more, stirring every five minutes. Let the casserole stand for 10 minutes before puréeing the mixture in batches in a blender or food processor. Return the purée to the casserole; then stir in the cream. Microwave the mixture on high until it is heated through — about two minutes.

In a bowl, microwave the remaining tablespoon of butter on high until it melts — about 30 seconds. Add the scallops and cook them on high for 30 seconds; stir the scallops, then cook them just until they turn opaque — about 30 seconds more.

Ladle the hot purée into heated individual soup plates; garnish each serving with some scallops and serve the soup immediately.

Cold Apple-and-Tarragon Soup

Serves 4
Working (and total) time: about 1 hour and 20 minutes
(includes chilling)

Calories **150**
Protein **4g.**
Cholesterol **9mg.**
Total fat **4g.**
Saturated fat **2g.**
Sodium **130mg.**

½ tbsp. unsalted butter
1 tbsp. finely chopped shallot
1¼ lb. tart apples, peeled, cored and sliced
2 tbsp. chopped fresh tarragon
1¼ cups unsalted chicken stock
¾ cup unsweetened apple juice
¼ tsp. white pepper
⅛ tsp. salt
grated nutmeg
1 cup low-fat milk
tarragon sprigs for garnish (optional)

Put the butter into a 2-quart bowl. Cover the bowl with plastic wrap or a lid, and microwave the butter on high until it has melted — about 30 seconds. Add the shallot and stir to coat it with the butter. Cover the bowl again and cook the shallot on medium high (70 percent power) until it is translucent — about 45 seconds. Add the apples, tarragon, stock, apple juice, pepper, salt and a pinch of nutmeg. Cover the bowl and cook the mixture on high until the apples are soft — about six minutes.

Purée the contents of the bowl in a blender, food processor or food mill. Return the soup to the bowl and refrigerate it for at least one hour, then stir in the milk. Garnish the soup with the tarragon sprigs, if you are using them, and serve immediately.

Chicken Ratatouille

Serves 4
Working (and total) time: about 45 minutes

Calories **240**
Protein **29g.**
Cholesterol **72mg.**
Total fat **5g.**
Saturated fat **1g.**
Sodium **345mg.**

¼ cup Madeira
2 tsp. chopped fresh oregano, or ½ tsp. dried oregano
1 tsp. chopped fresh rosemary, or ½ tsp. dried rosemary
1 tsp. chopped fresh thyme, or ¼ tsp. dried thyme leaves
2 tbsp. finely chopped shallot
2 garlic cloves, finely chopped
1 tsp. safflower oil
14 oz. canned unsalted tomatoes, puréed with their juice in a blender or food processor
1 small bay leaf
1 small eggplant (about 12 oz.), cut into 1-inch chunks
1 small zucchini, cut into 1-inch chunks
1 small yellow squash, cut into 1-inch chunks
1 sweet red pepper, seeded, deribbed and cut into 1-inch squares
1 green pepper, seeded, deribbed and cut into 1-inch squares
½ tsp. salt
freshly ground black pepper
1 lb. chicken breast meat, cut into ¾-inch cubes

Place the Madeira, oregano, rosemary and thyme in a cup and microwave them on high for two minutes. Set the cup aside and let it stand for five minutes.

Put the shallot and garlic into a 2-quart glass bowl; stir in the oil and microwave the mixture on medium (50 percent power) for two minutes. Add the tomato purée, bay leaf, eggplant, zucchini, squash, red pepper, green pepper and the herb mixture. Stir gently to distribute the vegetables, then cover the bowl with plastic wrap or a lid. Microwave the mixture on high for eight minutes, stirring once during the process.

Sprinkle the salt and some pepper over the chicken cubes, then stir them into the ratatouille. Cover the bowl and microwave it on high for five minutes, stirring once during the process. If the chicken is not white throughout, cook the ratatouille for one or two minutes more. Remove the bay leaf and transfer the ratatouille to a warmed serving dish. Serve immediately.

Glossary

Ancho chili pepper (also called Mexican chili pepper): the ripened and dried form of the poblano chili pepper. Dark reddish brown and mild to slightly hot, the ancho is the most commonly used chili in Mexico. See also Chili peppers.

Arugula (also called rocket, *roquette* and *rugula*): a peppery-flavored plant with long, leafy stems.

Balsamic vinegar: a mild, extremely fragrant wine-based vinegar made in Modena, Italy.

Bâtonnet (also called *bâton*): a vegetable piece that has been cut in the shape of a stick; bâtonnets are slightly larger than julienne.

Bay scallops: see Scallops.

Bean curd: see Tofu.

Bean paste (also called bean sauce): a thick brown paste made from soybeans, spices and salt.

Blanch: to immerse food briefly in boiling water. Blanching makes thin-skinned fruits and vegetables easier to peel; it can also mellow strong flavors and remove fat and impurities.

Bouquet garni: several herbs — the classic three are parsley, thyme and bay leaf — tied together or wrapped in cheesecloth, and used to flavor a stock or stew. The bouquet garni should be removed and discarded at the end of the cooking time.

Buttermilk: a tangy, low-fat cultured-milk product that can be used in cooking to replace richer ingredients.

Calorie (kilocalorie): a unit of heat measurement used to gauge the amount of energy a food supplies when it is broken down for use in the body.

Caramelize: to heat sugar, or a naturally sugar-rich food such as onion, until the sugar becomes brown and syrupy.

Cardamom: the bittersweet dried seeds of a plant in the ginger family. May be used whole or ground.

Casserole: a heavy, heat-absorbing pot, ideal for cooking soups and stews slowly. To prevent evaporation of the liquid, the casserole should have a tight lid. Earthenware or glass casseroles should be used only in the oven, never on the stove top.

Cayenne pepper: a fiery powder ground from the seeds and pods of various red chili peppers.

Celeriac (also called celery root): the knobby, tuberous root of a plant in the celery family.

Celery cabbage: an elongated cabbage with yellowish green leaves. See also Nappa cabbage.

Cellophane noodles (also called bean-thread noodles, glass noodles, *harusame, saifun* and transparent noodles): an Asian pasta made from various vegetable starches, most often that of mung beans. Cellophane noodles are available in forms ranging from 1-ounce skeins to 1-pound packages of loose noodles. Before cooking they should be soaked in hot water until they are soft.

Chervil: a lacy, slightly anise-flavored herb. Because long cooking may kill its flavor, chervil should be added at the last minute.

Chiffonade: a leafy vegetable sliced into very thin shreds.

Chili peppers: a variety of hot red or green pepper. Fresh or dried, chili peppers contain volatile oils that can irritate the skin and eyes; they must be handled with extreme care *(caution, page 95)*. See also Ancho chili pepper, Jalapeño chili pepper.

Chinese five-spice powder (also called five heavenly spices and five fragrant spices): a pungent blend of ground spices, most often fennel seeds, star anise, cloves, cinnamon or cassia, and Sichuan peppercorns; it should be used sparingly. If five-spice powder is unavailable, substitute a mixture of equal parts ground Sichuan peppercorns, cloves, cinnamon and fennel seeds.

Chinese parsley: see Cilantro.

Cholesterol: a waxy, fatlike substance that is manufactured in the human body and is also found in foods of animal origin. Although a certain amount of cholesterol is necessary for proper body functioning, an excess can accumulate in the arteries, contributing to heart disease. See also Monounsaturated fats; Polyunsaturated fats; Saturated fats.

Cilantro (also called fresh coriander and Chinese parsley): the fresh leaves of the coriander plant; cilantro imparts a lemony, pleasingly pungent flavor to many Latin American, Indian and Asian dishes.

Cloud-ear mushrooms (also called tree ears, tree fungus, mo-er and wood ears): flavorless lichen used primarily for their crunchy texture and dark color. Cloud ears expand more than other mushrooms when soaked. See also Mushrooms, dried Asian.

Coconut milk, unsweetened: a liquid extracted from fresh or dried coconut meat. Unsweetened coconut milk can be purchased either canned or frozen; because of its high saturated-fat content, it should be used sparingly.

Coriander seeds: the earthy-tasting seeds of the coriander plant, often used as an ingredient in curries. See also Cilantro.

Couscous: a fine-grained semolina pasta, traditionally served as a base for the classic North African stew of the same name.

Crystallized ginger (also called candied ginger): stems of young ginger preserved with sugar. Crystallized ginger should not be confused with ginger in syrup.

Cumin: the seeds of a plant related to caraway. Raw, the seeds add a pleasant bitterness to curry powder and chili powder; toasted, they have a nutty taste.

Dark sesame oil: a dark seasoning oil, high in polyunsaturated fats, that is made from toasted sesame seeds. Because the oil has a low smoking point, it is rarely heated. Dark sesame oil should not be confused or replaced with lighter sesame cooking oils.

Deglaze: to dissolve the brown particles left in a pan after roasting or sautéing by stirring in a liquid such as wine, stock, water or cream.

Degrease: to remove fat from the surface of stock or a cooking liquid. See also box, page 55.

Dice: to cut a food into small cubes of equal size.

Dijon mustard: a smooth mustard once manufactured only in Dijon, France; it may be flavored with herbs, green peppercorns or white wine.

Fat: a basic component of many foods, comprising three types of fat — saturated, monounsaturated and polyunsaturated — in varying proportions. See also Monounsaturated fats; Polyunsaturated fats; Saturated fats.

Fennel (also called Florence fennel and finocchio): a vegetable with feathery green tops and a thick, bulbous stalk. It has a milky, licorice flavor; the tops are used both as a garnish and as a flavoring. Fennel is sometimes incorrectly labeled anise.

Fennel seeds: the aromatic dried seeds from herb fennel, a relative of vegetable fennel; they are used as a licorice-flavored seasoning in many Italian dishes. The seeds are also used in curries and to make Chinese five-spice powder.

Fermented black beans: soybeans that have been fermented, dried and salted.

Fish sauce (also called *nuoc mam* and *nam pla*): a thin, brown, salty liquid made from fermented fish and used in Southeast Asian cooking to bring out the flavors of a dish.

Ginger: the spicy, buff-colored, rootlike stem of the ginger plant, used as a seasoning either fresh, or dried and powdered. See also Crystallized ginger.

Harissa: a fiery-hot North African condiment, based on red chili peppers. Sambal oelek, an Indonesian chili paste, may be used in its place.

Hoisin sauce (also called Haisein sauce and Beijing sauce): a thick, dark reddish brown, soybean-based Chinese condiment. Its flavor is at once sweet and spicy.

Hot red-pepper sauce: a hot, unsweetened chili sauce, such as Tabasco sauce.

Italian parsley: a flat-leaved parsley with a more pronounced flavor than curly-leaved parsley.

Jalapeño chili pepper: a squat, green, hot chili pepper, essential to a number of Mexican dishes. See also Chili peppers.

Jícama: a brown-skinned globular root weighing one to six pounds. Its white flesh is delicately sweet and stays crunchy even after cooking.

Julienne: to slice into matchstick-size pieces; also the name for the pieces themselves.

Juniper berry: the berry of the juniper tree, used as a key flavoring in gin as well as in pork dishes and sauerkraut. Whole juniper berries should be removed from a dish before it is served.

Lemon grass (citronella): a long, woody, lemon-flavored stalk that is shaped like a scallion. Lemon grass is available in Asian markets. To store it, refrigerate it in plastic wrap for up to two weeks or freeze it for as long as three months.

Lily buds (also called golden needles): the dried buds of the day lily, used in Chinese dishes for their tangy, smoky flavor. The buds must be softened by soaking before use.

Mexican oregano: any of several Mexican varieties of a pungent herb unrelated botanically to the Mediterranean species.

Mirin: a sweetened Japanese cooking wine that is made from rice. If mirin is unavailable, substitute white wine or saké mixed with a little sugar.

Monounsaturated fat: one of the three components of food fat. Monounsaturated fats are believed not to raise the level of cholesterol in the blood. Some oils high in monounsaturated fats — olive oil, for example — may even lower the cholesterol level.

Mushrooms, dried Asian: any of several fungi often used in Asian cooking. Before use, dried Asian mushrooms must be covered with boiling water and soaked for at least 20 minutes, then trimmed of their woody stems. To convert the mushroom-soaking liquid into a flavoring agent, let the sand settle out, then pour off and reserve the clear liquid. See also Cloud-ear mushrooms; Shiitake mushrooms.

Nappa cabbage (also called Chinese cabbage): an elongated cabbage resembling romaine lettuce, with long, broad ribs and crinkled, light-green to white leaves. Often confused with celery cabbage, which is more elongated and has broader-ribbed leaves.

Nonreactive pan: a cooking vessel whose surface does not react with the acids in food. The surface may be stainless steel, enamel, glass or an alloy. Untreated cast iron and aluminum may react with acids, producing discoloration or a peculiar taste.

Okra: the green pods of a plant indigenous to Africa, where it is called gumbo. In stews, okra is prized for its thickening properties.

Olive oil: any of various grades of cooking oil extracted from olives. Extra virgin olive oil has a full, fruity flavor and the lowest acidity. Virgin olive oil is slightly higher in acidity. Pure olive oil, a processed blend of olive oils, has the highest acidity.

Orzo: a rice-shaped pasta made of semolina.

Poach: to cook a food in barely simmering liquid.

Polyunsaturated fat: one of the three types of fat found in foods, existing in abundance in such vegetable oils as safflower, sunflower, corn and soybean. Polyunsaturated fats actually lower the level of cholesterol in the blood.

Purée: to reduce food to a smooth consistency by forcing it through a sieve or a food mill, or by processing it in a blender or food processor.

Recommended Dietary Allowance (RDA): the average daily amount of an essential nutrient as determined for groups of healthy people of various ages by the National Research Council.

Reduce: to boil down a liquid in order to concentrate its flavor or thicken its consistency.

Rice vinegar: a mild, fragrant vinegar that is less sweet than cider vinegar and not as harsh as distilled white vinegar. Japanese rice vinegar is milder than the Chinese variety.

Roll-cut: to slice a cylindrical vegetable, such as a carrot or an asparagus stalk, by rolling it a quarter of a turn between diagonal slices. The decorative pieces that result offer increased surface area for seasonings.

Rutabaga: a cruciferous root vegetable that resembles a large turnip but has reddish brown skin and yellow flesh.

Safflower oil: vegetable oil that contains the highest proportion of polyunsaturated fats.

Saffron: the dried, yellowish red stigmas (or threads) of the flower of *Crocus sativus;* they yield a slightly bitter flavor and a brilliant yellow color. Powdered saffron may be substituted for the threads, but it is less flavorful.

Saturated fats: one of the three components of food fat. Found in abundance in animal products and in coconut and palm oils, saturated fats raise the level of cholesterol in the blood. Because a high blood-cholesterol level is a risk factor for heart disease, saturated-fat consumption should be held to less than 10 percent of the calories in a daily diet.

Savoy cabbage: a variety of head cabbage with a mild flavor and crisp, crinkly leaves.

Scallion (also called green onion and spring onion): a slender member of the onion family, with a white base supporting elongated green leaves.

Scallop: a bivalve mollusk. The cylindrical adductor muscle of the animal is the part usually eaten by Americans, although the orange roe is edible too. The bay scallop, harvested from Cape Cod to Cape Hatteras, measures about ½ inch in diameter. The smaller calico scallop, sometimes mislabeled "bay scallop," is found from the Carolinas to Brazil. Sea scallops measure up to 2½ inches in diameter.

Sesame oil: see Dark sesame oil.

Sesame seeds: pale, hulled or unhulled seeds that are a good source of calcium. To toast sesame seeds, cook them in a dry skillet over low heat, stirring or shaking the pan gently to prevent burning, until the seeds are golden.

Shallot: a mild variety of onion, with a subtle flavor and papery, red-brown skin.

Shank (veal, beef or lamb): the shin portion of the animal's leg.

Shiitake mushrooms: a variety of mushroom, originally cultivated only in Japan, that is sold fresh or dried. The dried form should be soaked and stemmed before use. See also Mushrooms, dried Asian.

Sichuan pepper (also called Chinese pepper, Japanese pepper and anise pepper): the dried berry of a shrub native to China. Its flavor is tart, aromatic and less piquant than that of black pepper. To toast Sichuan peppercorns, cook them in a dry skillet over low heat, gently shaking the pan to prevent burning, until the peppercorns are fragrant.

Simmer: to cook a liquid or sauce just below its boiling point so that the liquid's surface barely trembles.

Snow peas: flat green pea pods that are eaten whole, with only the stems and strings removed.

Sodium: a nutrient essential to maintaining the proper balance of fluids in the body. In most diets, a major source of the element is table salt, containing 40 percent sodium. Excess sodium may cause high blood pressure, which is a contributor to heart disease. One teaspoon of salt, with 2,132 milligrams of sodium, contains about two thirds of the maximum "safe and adequate" daily sodium intake recommended by the National Research Council.

Soy sauce: a savory, salty brown liquid made from fermented soybeans, available in both light- and dark-colored variations. One tablespoon of regular soy sauce contains 1,030 milligrams of sodium; lower-sodium variations may contain half that amount.

Stock: a savory liquid made by simmering aromatic vegetables, herbs and spices — and usually meat, bones and trimmings — in water *(recipes, pages 10-11).* Stock forms a flavor-rich base for soups and stews.

Sweet chili sauce: any of a group of Asian sauces containing chilies, vinegar, garlic, sugar and salt. The sauce may be used as a condiment to accompany meats, poultry or fish, or it may be included as an ingredient in a dish.

Tamarind (also called Indian date): the pulp surrounding the seeds of the tamarind plant, yielding a juice that is considerably more sour than lemon juice. Grown and used throughout Asia, tamarind is available fresh, in pod form, in bricks or as concentrate.

Tofu (also called bean curd): a dense, custard-like soybean product with a mild flavor. It is rich in protein, relatively low in calories and free of cholesterol.

Tomatillo: a small, tart, green, tomato-like fruit vegetable that is used frequently in Mexican dishes. It is covered with an inedible, loose, papery husk.

Total fat: an individual's daily intake of polyunsaturated, monounsaturated and saturated fats. Nutritionists recommend that fat constitute no more than 30 percent of the calories in a diet. The term as applied in this book refers to the combined fats in a given dish or food.

Veal breast: the flavorful breast portion of a calf. Veal breast contains gelatinous material that melts during long simmering, lending body to its cooking liquid.

Virgin olive oil: see Olive oil.

Water chestnut: the walnut-size tuber of an aquatic Asian plant, with rough brown skin and sweet, crisp white flesh. Fresh water chestnuts may be refrigerated for up to two weeks; they must be peeled before use. To store canned water chestnuts, first blanch or rinse them, then refrigerate them for as long as three weeks in fresh water changed daily. A crisp, mild vegetable such as jícama or Jerusalem artichoke makes an acceptable substitute.

White pepper: a powder ground from the same dried berry as that used to make black pepper, but with the berry's outer shell removed before grinding, resulting in a milder flavor. Ground white pepper is used as a less visible alternative to black pepper in light-colored foods.

Zest: the flavorful outermost layer of citrus-fruit rind, cut or grated free of the bitter white pith that lies beneath it.

Index

A corn squash soup, gingery, 132
Apples:
 Escarole soup with turnips and, 40
 Soup with tarragon, 138
 Stew of pork and, 110
Apricots, beef stew, couscous and, 116
Artichoke and mussel chowder, 77
Asparagus-and-crab soup, Vietnamese, 85
Avocado soup, dilly, 19

B ass, striped, soup with sweet pepper, 71

Beans:
 Black, soup with bourbon and ham, 15
 Red, stew with squid, 123
 White, soup with garlic, 42
Bean-sprout and pork soup, 135
Beef:
 Chili, chunky, 94
 Soup
  with Brussels sprouts and sweet potato, 61
  with capellini, 52
  with wild mushrooms, 67
 Stew
  with apricots and couscous, 116
  sauerbraten, with candied ginger, 113
  with stout, 114
  with tangerines, 101
Beet and parsnip soup, 27
Black bean, bourbon and ham soup, 15
Black-eyed pea and collard green soup, 25
Bouillon, court, 69
Bourbon, black bean and ham soup, 15
Bread soup, 17
Broccoli soup with cumin and bay scallops, 137
Brown stock, 11
Brunoise, 51

Brussels sprouts, beef soup with sweet potato and, 61
Buttermilk soup, curried, with zucchini, 20

C abbage:
 Nappa
  chicken soup with, 60
  pork soup with, 61
 Soup with caraway, 34
Capellini, beef soup with, 52
Caraway:
 Soup with cabbage, 34
 Soup with celeriac, 39

Caribbean red-snapper stew, 123
Carrots:
    Garnish of, 50
    Oxtail stew with, 111
    Roll-cutting, 112
    Soup
        chicken, 53
        cream, 46
        oyster with watercress, 72
Cauliflower soup:
    Provençale, 37
    puréed, 36
Celeriac soup, caraway-flavored, 39
Celery:
    Dumplings with lemon in turkey
        soup, 66
    Soup with leek and Gruyère, 20
Cheese:
    Gruyère, leek and celery soup, 20
    Ricotta stars, tomato purée with, 22
    Roquefort onion soup, 45
Chestnut soup, 43
Chicken:
    Grilled, vegetable soup with, 64
    Ratatouille, 138
    Soup
        with carrots, potatoes and
            spinach, 53
        with chilies and cabbage, 60
        with eggplant and tomato, 59
    Stew
        gumbo, 97
        with mashed potatoes, 136
        Mexican, with ancho chilies, 108
        in peppers, 114
        ratatouille, 138
        simmered in sake, 56
        with zucchini and tomatoes, 100
    Stock, 10
Chiffonade, 51
Chili:
    Beef, chunky, 94
    Seafood, with peppers and
        tomatillos, 128
Chilies:
    Cautions about, 95
    Chicken soup with cabbage and, 60
    Chicken stew with, 108
Chowder:
    Conch, Key West, 70
    Fish, Mediterranean, 120
    Mussel and artichoke, 77
Cilantro and corn soup, 33
Clam and rice soup, 72
Clarifying stock, 49
Cod stewed with vegetables, 119
Collard green and black-eyed pea
    soup, 25
Conch chowder, Key West, 70
Consommé, 49
    Degreasing, 55
    Garnishes for, 50-51
Corn:
    Soup with cilantro, 33
    Soup with scallops and fettuccine, 84
Court bouillon, 69
Couscous:
    Beef stew with apricots and, 116
    Soup with harissa, 68
Crab:
    Soup with asparagus, 85
    Soup with tomato and fennel, 69
Cream of carrot soup with ginger, 46
Creole, shrimp, 124
Croutons, 9

Cucumbers:
    Sauce with yogurt, 92
    Soup, curried, 46
Cumin, broccoli soup with scallops
    and, 137
Curry:
    Soup
        buttermilk and zucchini, 20
        cucumber, chilled, 46
        vegetable, cold, 31
        yellow split pea, with lamb and
            mint, 39
    Stew
        flounder, 125
        lamb with tamarind, Java, 99

*D*egreasing, 55
Dilly avocado soup, 19
Duck:
    Skinning, 55
    Soup with endive and pears, 54
    Stew with watercress, 106
Dumplings:
    Lemon-celery, turkey soup with, 66
    Seafood, hot and sweet soup with,
        80

*E*ast Indian vegetable stew, 92
Eggplant, chicken and tomato soup, 59
Endive, duck soup with pears and, 54
Escarole soup with turnips and apple,
    40

*F*at, removing, from liquids, 55
Fennel, crab and tomato soup, 69
Fettuccine, corn and scallop soup, 84
Fine kettle of fish, a, 81
Fish. *See individual names*
Fish and shellfish soup:
    Clam and rice, 72
    Crab, fennel and tomato, 69
    Crab-and-asparagus, Vietnamese, 85
    Fish
        a fine kettle of, 81
        with red-pepper sauce, 78
        and spinach, 74
    Key West conch chowder, 70
    Mussel and artichoke chowder, 77
    Oyster, with leeks, 79
    Oyster, with watercress and carrot,
        72
    Salmon, smoked, green pea soup
        with, 26
    Scallop
        broccoli, with cumin, 137
        with corn and fettuccine, 84
        with 20 garlic cloves, 75
    Seafood-dumpling, hot and sweet,
        80
    Shrimp, chilled, with tomato, 76
    Shrimp with lemon grass, Thai, 82
    Striped bass and sweet pepper, 71
Fish and shellfish stew:
    Chili with peppers and tomatillos,
        128
    Cod, with vegetables, 119
    Flounder curry, 125
    Gumbo, Southwest, 118
    Lobster navarin, 127
    Mediterranean chowder, 120
    Red-snapper, Caribbean, 123
    Salmon, in red wine, 121

Seafood, in garlic-tomato sauce, 135
Seafood, with water chestnuts, 117
Shrimp creole, 124
Squid and red-bean, 123
Sweet-and-sour, 133
Trout, with vegetables, 126
Fish stock, 11
Flounder curry, 125

*G*arlic:
    Sauce, tomato, 135
    Soup with
        scallop, 75
        white bean, 42
Garnishes, 9, 50-51
Gazpacho:
    Blanco, 29
    Golden, 86
    With roasted peppers, 44
Ginger:
    Acorn squash soup with, 132
    Candied, sauerbraten stew with, 113
    Cream of carrot soup with, 46
    Pear soup with, 86
Granita, tomato, 33
Green pea soup with smoked salmon,
    26
Gruyère, leek and celery soup, 20
Gumbo:
    Chicken, 97
    Southwest, 118

*H*am, black bean and bourbon soup,
    15
Harissa, couscous soup with, 68
Hot and sour soup, 35
Hot and sweet soup with seafood
    dumplings, 80

*L*amb:
    Curry with tamarind, Java, 99
    Soup
        split pea and mint, curried, 39
        with wild rice, 58
        with winter vegetables, 63
    Stew with spinach and orzo, 107
Leeks:
    Soup with celery and Gruyère, 20
    Soup with oysters, 79
Lemon-celery dumplings, 66
Lemon grass, Thai shrimp soup with, 82
Lentils:
    Soup, turkey, 62
    Stew, sausage, 95
Lobster navarin, 127

*M*icrowave recipes, 131-138
    Soup
        broccoli, with cumin and bay
            scallops, 137
        cold apple-and-tarragon, 138
        gingery acorn squash, 132
        pork and bean-sprout, 135
    Stew
        chicken, with potatoes, 136
        chicken ratatouille, 138
        seafood, in garlic-tomato sauce,
            135
        sweet-and-sour fish, 133
        vegetable, with snow peas and
            mustard, 131

Minestrone, vegetable-broth, 28
Mint, curried split pea soup with lamb
    and, 39
Mushroom soup:
    With beef, 67
    With sherry, 18
Mussel and artichoke chowder, 77
Mustard:
    Veal stew with pearl onions and, 108
    Vegetable stew with snow peas and,
        131

*N*appa cabbage:
    Chicken soup with, 60
    Pork soup with, 61
Navarin, lobster, 127
Noodle and veal soup with sage, 56
Nutritional information, 7, 8, *chart* 8

*O*ils, 8
Okra, vegetable stew with, 91
Onions:
    Pearl, veal stew with mustard and, 108
    Soup, Roquefort, 45
    Soup with red potatoes and walnut
        toasts, 30
Orzo, lamb-spinach stew with, 107
Oxtails braised with carrots, 111
Oyster soup:
    With leeks, 79
    With watercress and carrot, 72

*P*arsley soup, cold, with tomato
    granita, 33
Parsnip and beet soup, 27
Peach soup flambé, 87
Peanut soup, peppery, 41
Pears:
    Soup, duck, with endive, 54
    Soup, gingery, 86
Peas:
    Black-eyed, soup with collard greens
        and, 25
    Green, soup with smoked salmon
        and, 26
    Snow, vegetable stew with mustard
        and, 131
    Yellow split, curried soup with lamb
        and mint, 39
Peppers:
    Chili
        cautions about, 95
        chicken soup with cabbage and, 60
        chicken stew with, 108
    Sweet
        beef and capellini soup, 52
        chicken stew in, 114
        gazpacho with, 44
        sauce, fish soup with, 78
        sauce, turkey stew with, 96
        seafood chili with, 128
        soup with striped bass, 71
        veal stew with, 102
Pork:
    Soup
        with bean sprouts, 135
        with Nappa cabbage, 61
    Stew with apples, 110
Potatoes:
    Chicken soup with carrots, spinach
        and, 53
    Mashed, chicken stew with, 136

Soup with onions and walnut toasts, 30
Sweet
soup with beef and Brussels sprouts, 61
soup with vegetables, 16
stew, 92
Prunes, rabbit stew with, 103
Puréeing, 20

*R*abbit stew:
With prunes, 103
With sherry, 105
Ratatouille, chicken, 138
Recommended Dietary Guidelines, *chart* 8
Rice:
Chicken soup with, 60
Clam soup with, 72
Wild, soup with lamb, 58
Ricotta-yogurt stars, tomato purée with, 22
Roll-cutting vegetables, 112
Roquefort onion soup, 45

*S*age, veal and noodle soup with, 56
Sake, velvet chicken soup simmered in, 56
Salmon:
In red wine, 121
Smoked, green pea soup with, 26
Sauces:
Cucumber-yogurt, 92
Garlic-tomato, 135
Red-pepper
for fish soup, 78
for turkey stew, 96
Sauerbraten stew with candied ginger, 113
Sausage-lentil stew, 95
Scallions, soup with, 23
Beef and capellini, 52
Scallops, soup with:
Broccoli, with cumin, 137
With corn and fettuccine, 84
With garlic, 75
Seafood. *See also individual names*
Chili with peppers and tomatillos, 128
Dumplings, hot and sweet soup with, 80
Soup, 81
Stew
with garlic-tomato sauce, 135
with water chestnuts, 117
Shallot soup, caramelized, 14
Sherry:
Mushroom soup with, 18
Rabbit stew with, 105
Vegetable potpourri with, 90
Shrimp:
Creole, 124
Soup
Thai, with lemon grass, 82
with tomato, 76
Snapper, red, Caribbean stew, 123
Snow peas, vegetable stew with mustard and, 131
Soups, 7, 9, 13
Acorn squash, gingery, 132
Avocado, with dill, 19
Bean
black, with bourbon and ham, 15
white, with garlic, 42

Beef
with Brussels sprouts and sweet potato, 61
with capellini, 52
with wild mushrooms, 67
Beet and parsnip, 27
Black-eyed pea and collard green, 25
Bread, 17
Buttermilk and zucchini, curried, 20
Cabbage and caraway, 34
Carrot, cream of, with ginger, 46
Cauliflower
Provençale, 37
puréed, 36
Celeriac, with caraway, 39
Chestnut, 43
Chicken
with carrots, potatoes and spinach, 53
with chilies and cabbage, 60
with eggplant and tomato, 59
velvet, with sake, 56
Cold
apple-and-tarragon, 138
avocado, with dill, 19
curried cucumber, 46
curried vegetable, 31
gazpacho, golden, 86
gazpacho blanco, 29
gazpacho with peppers, 44
parsley, with tomato granita, 33
shrimp and tomato, 76
sweet potato and vegetable, 16
tarragon-zucchini, 24
Consommé, 49
degreasing, 55
garnishes for, 50-51
Corn and cilantro, 33
Couscous, with harissa, 68
Cucumber, curried, 46
Duck, with endive and pears, 54
Escarole, with turnips and apple, 40
Fish (*see* Fish and shellfish soup)
Gazpacho
blanco, 29
golden, 86
with peppers, 44
Green pea, with smoked salmon, 26
Hot and sour, 35
Hot and sweet, with seafood dumplings, 80
Lamb
with wild rice, 58
with winter vegetables, 63
Leek, celery and Gruyère, 20
Minestrone, vegetable-broth, 28
Mushroom, with sherry, 18
Onion, Roquefort, 45
Onion and potato, with walnut toasts, 30
Parsley, cold, with tomato granita, 33
Peach, flambé, 87
Peanut, peppery, 41
Pear, gingery, 86
Pork, with Nappa cabbage, 61
Pork and bean-sprout, 135
Scallion, 23
Shallot, caramelized, 14
Split pea, with lamb and mint, curried, 39
Sweet potato and vegetable, 16
Tarragon-zucchini, 24
Tomato, with yogurt-ricotta stars, 22
Turkey
goulash, 65

with lemon-celery dumplings, 66
lentil, 62
Turnip, 48
Veal and noodle, with sage, 56
Vegetable
cold curried, 31
with grilled chicken, 64
lamb, 63
minestrone, 28
with sweet potatoes, 16
Spinach:
Chicken soup with, 53
Fish soup with, 74
Lamb stew with orzo and, 107
Split pea soup with lamb and mint, curried, 39
Squash. *See* Acorn squash; Zucchini
Squid and red-bean stew, 123
Stews, 7, 9, 89
Beef
with apricots and couscous, 116
chili, chunky, 94
sauerbraten, with ginger, 113
with stout, 114
with tangerines, 101
Chicken
with ancho chilies, Mexican, 108
gumbo, 97
with mashed potatoes, 136
in peppers, 114
ratatouille, 138
with zucchini and tomatoes, 100
Duck, with watercress, 106
Fish. *See* Fish and shellfish stew
Lamb
curry with tamarind, Java, 99
with spinach and orzo, 107
Lentil-sausage, 95
Oxtail, with carrots, 111
Pork and apple, 110
Rabbit
with prunes, 103
with sherry, 105
Sauerbraten, with candied ginger, 113
Sweet potato, 92
Turkey, with Mediterranean vegetables, 96
Veal
with pearl onions and mustard, 108
with peppers, 102
Vegetable
East Indian, 92
with okra, 91
sherried, 90
with snow peas and mustard, 131
Stock, 7, 10-11
Clarifying, 49
Stout, beef stew with, 114
Striped bass and sweet pepper soup, 71
Sweet-and-sour fish stew, 133
Sweet potatoes:
Soup with beef and Brussels sprouts, 61
Soup with vegetables, 16
Stew, 92

*T*amarind, Java lamb curry with, 99
Tangerine beef stew, 101
Tarragon, soup with:
Apple, 138
Zucchini, 24
Thai shrimp soup with lemon grass, 82
Tomatillos, seafood chili with, 128

Tomatoes:
Chicken stew with zucchini and, 100
Garnish of, 50
Granita, 33
Sauce with garlic, 135
Soup
with chicken and eggplant, 59
with crab and fennel, 69
with shrimp, 76
with yogurt-ricotta stars, 22
Tortilla-strip garnish, 64
Trout stew with vegetables, 126
Turkey:
Soup
goulash, 65
with lemon-celery dumplings, 66
lentil, 62
Stew with Mediterranean vegetables, 96
Turning vegetables, 128
Turnips, soup with, 48
Escarole and apple, 40

*V*eal:
Noodle soup with sage, 56
Stew
with pearl onions and mustard, 108
with sweet peppers, 102
Stock, 10
Vegetables. *See also individual names*
Garnishes of, for consommé, 50-51
Soup
cold curried, 31
with grilled chicken, 64
lamb, 63
minestrone, 28
sweet potato, 16
Stew
cod, 119
East Indian, 92
with mustard, 131
with okra, 91
sherried, 90
with trout, 126
turkey with Mediterranean vegetables, 96
Stock, 10
Velvet chicken soup with sake, 56
Vietnamese crab-and-asparagus soup, 85

*W*alnut toasts, onion and potato soup with, 30
Water chestnuts, seafood stew with, 117
Watercress:
Duck stew with, 106
Oyster soup with carrot and, 72
White bean soup with garlic, 42
Wine, red, salmon stew in, 121

*Y*ogurt:
Ricotta stars on tomato purée, 22
Sauce with cucumber, 92

*Z*ucchini:
Chicken stew with tomatoes and, 100
Soup
curried, with buttermilk, 20
with tarragon, 24

Picture Credits

All photographs in this volume were taken by staff photographer Renée Comet unless otherwise indicated below:

2: top and center, Carolyn Wall Rothery. 5: lower right, Taran Z. 9: Taran Z. 16: bottom, Michael Latil. 20: Steven Biver. 23: top, Michael Latil. 25: Steven Biver. 31, 32: Michael Latil. 33: Aldo Tutino. 37: bottom, Michael Latil. 38-43: Steven Biver. 45: Steven Biver. 49: top, Michael Latil; bottom, Taran Z. 50-51: Taran Z. 55: Taran Z. 57: Michael Latil. 61: bottom, Michael Latil. 63: Michael Latil. 70: Michael Latil. 90, 91: Michael Latil. 93: Michael Latil. 97: Taran Z. 103-105: Michael Latil. 107: Taran Z. 109: Michael Latil. 112: upper left, Taran Z; lower left, Michael Latil. 114, 115: Taran Z. 118: Taran Z. 121: Michael Latil. 123: Michael Latil. 125: Michael Latil. 127, 128: Taran Z. 130: Taran Z. 133, 134: Taran Z. 136-138: Taran Z.

Props: Cover: Deruta of Italy, Corp., New York. 6: pitcher, Country Lace Antiques, Bowie, Md.; crocks, Frederick B. Hanson Country Antiques, Keedysville, Md.; cutting board and knife, The Peddler's Wagon, Middletown, Md. 12-13: Nancy Brucks. 14: Cherishables Antiques, Washington, D.C. 15: rear bowl, Skellin and Company, Bethesda, Md. 16: Gertrude Berman. 17: Williams-Sonoma, Washington, D.C. 19: briefcase, Marty Block. 20: plate, ECCO Cafe & Pizzaria, Alexandria, Va.; bowl, The Pineapple Country Collection, Alexandria, Va. 22: Manhattan Ad Hoc, New York. 23: Luna Garcia, Venice, Calif. 25: The Olde Country Cupboard, Funkstown, Md. 26:

Stanley Andersen, The American Hand Plus, Washington, D.C. 27: Micheline's Country French Antiques, Alexandria, Va. 29: Terrafirma Ceramics, Inc., New York. 31: Evergreen Antiques, New York. 32: tablecloth, A Bit of Britain, Alexandria, Va. 34: King Street Antiques, Alexandria, Va. 35: Rob Barnard, Timberville, Va. 36: Mark Anderson, Torpedo Factory Art Center, Alexandria, Va. 37: Skellin and Company. 38: Nancy Brucks. 39: Skellin and Company, 40: Phyllis Van Auken Antiques, Kensington, Md. 41: Beth Armour, Putney, Vt. 42: Ellen Godwin. 43: Full Circle, Alexandria, Va. 44: fabric, Williams-Sonoma. 46: Jane Wilner, Washington, D.C. 47: Cherishables Antiques. 48: Cherishables Antiques. 50-51: Martin's of Georgetown, Washington, D.C. 52: Rob Barnard. 53: Full Circle. 54: Malcolm Wright, Marlboro, Vt. 57: Ginza "Things Japanese," Washington, D.C. 58: background, Michael Latil. 59: Jane Wilner. 60: strainer, Williams-Sonoma. 61: bottom, Evergreen Antiques. 63: copper pot, Marie A. Evans Antiques, Alexandria, Va. 65: Marston Luce Antiques, Washington, D.C. 66: Kate Brantley Augustus. 67: The Mediterranean Shop, New York. 68: Skellin and Company. 69: Elayne De Vito. 70: Barneys New York, New York. 71: Elayne De Vito; background, Wicker World, Washington, D.C. 72: Mara Superior, East Street Clay Studio, Hadley, Mass. 75: Taeko Wu. 76: Cherub Antiques Gallery, Georgetown Antiques Center, Washington, D.C. 78: Susan Greenleaf, Fire One, Torpedo Factory Art Center. 79: Jane Wilner. 80: Lois and Jesse Walden, Berkeley, Calif. 81: Geff Reed, The American Hand Plus. 84: Marston Luce Antiques. 85: Gary Sloane, The American Hand Plus.

86: left, Nambé Mills Inc., Santa Fe, N. Mex.; pears, Marston Luce Antiques; right, Williams-Sonoma. 87: Skellin and Company. 88-89: Marie A. Evans Antiques. 90: Susquehanna Antique Co. Inc., Washington, D.C. 91: Cliff Lee, Lee Gallery, Washington, D.C. 92: Skellin and Company. 93: The Kellogg Collection, Washington, D.C. 94: Williams-Sonoma. 98-99: background, Sharon Farrington. 102: Skellin and Company; spoon, Retroneu, New York. 103: American Country Antiques, Washington, D.C. 104-105: recipe file, Philip S. Stockslager. 107: Betty Gaines Alexandria Antiques, Alexandria, Va. 108: Dennis Davis, Waterfront Potters, Torpedo Factory Art Center. 109: Dennis Davis, Waterfront Potters, Torpedo Factory Art Center. 110: Victoria and Richard MacKenzie-Childs, Ltd., Aurora, N.Y. 111: Deruta of Italy, Corp. 112-113: Gigi Wirtz. 115: Barbara Eigen, Jane Wilner. 116: Kit Vorhaus, Waterfront Potters, Torpedo Factory Art Center. 117: The Kellogg Collection. 120: Royal Copenhagen Porcelain Corp., White Plains, N.Y. 121: Bruce Gholson, The American Hand Plus. 122: bowls, Mimi Harrison; plates, Skellin and Company. 123: The Kellogg Collection. 124: Susquehanna Antique Co., Inc. 125: skillet, Williams-Sonoma. 126: Susie Cohen, Alexandria, Va. 127: Marie A. Evans Antiques. 130: Limor Carrigan, Crofton, Md. 132: Barbara WF Miner, Columbus, Ohio. 133: Ginza "Things Japanese." 134: Susie Cohen. 135: The Mediterranean Shop. 136: rear casserole, Dennis Davis, Waterfront Potters, Torpedo Factory Art Center. 137: Lenore & Daughters, Alexandria, Va. 138: Uzzolo, Washington, D.C. 139: The Kellogg Collection.

Acknowledgments

The index for this book was prepared by Dick Mudrow. The editors are particularly indebted to the following people for creating recipes for this volume: Leslie Bloom, Silver Spring, Md.; Ellen Brown, Washington, D.C.; Nora Carey, Paris; Robert Carmack, Camas, Wash.; Robert Chambers, New York; Sharon Farrington, Bethesda, Md.; Rebecca Marshall, New York; Vivian Portner, Silver Spring, Md.; Christine Schuyler, Washington, D.C.; Jane Sigal, Paris; Lyn Stallworth, Brooklyn, N.Y.

The editors also wish to thank: The Amber Grain, Washington, D.C.; Ava Baker, Walpole, Mass.; Martha Blacksall, BBH Corporation, Washington, D.C.; Jo Calabrese, Royal Worcester Spode Inc., New York;

Nick Chantiles, Rockville, Md.; Nic Colling, Home Produce Company, Alexandria, Va.; Jeanne Dale, The Pilgrim Glass Corp., New York; Paul Dexter, Salvatore Termini, Deruta of Italy Corp., New York; Rex Downey, Oxon Hill, Md.; Dr. Jacob Exler, U.S. Department of Agriculture, Hyattsville, Md.; Flowers Unique, Alexandria, Va.; Dennis Garrett, Ed Nash, The American Hand Plus, Washington, D.C.; Giant Food, Inc., Landover, Md.; E. Goodwin & Sons, Inc., Jessup, Md.; Chong Su Han, Grass Roots Restaurant, Alexandria, Va.; Wretha Hanson, Franz Bader Gallery, Washington, D.C.; Steven Himmelfarb, U.S. Fish, Inc., Kensington, Md.; Imperial Produce, Washington, D.C.; Ann Kavaljian, Alexandria, Va.; Gary Latzman, Kirk Phillips, Retroneu, New York; Patricia Cassidy Lewis, Lorton, Va.; Dr. Richard Mattes, Monell Chemical

Senses Center, Philadelphia, Pa.; Nambé Mills Inc., Santa Fe, N. Mex.; Dr. Joyce Nettleton, Lexington, Mass.; Dr. Alfred C. Olson, U.S. Department of Agriculture, Albany, Calif.; Lisa Ownby, Alexandria, Va.; Joyce Piotrowski, Vienna, Va.; Linda Robertson, JUD Tile, Vienna, Va.; Safeway Stores, Inc., Landover, Md.; St. John's Herb Garden, Inc., Bowie, Md.; Bert Saunders, WILTON Armetale, New York; Straight from the Crate, Inc., Alexandria, Va.; Sutton Place Gourmet, Washington, D.C.; Kathy Swekel, Columbia, Md.; Williams-Sonoma, Washington, D.C. The editors wish to thank the following for their donation of kitchen equipment: Le Creuset, distributed by Schiller & Asmus, Inc., Yemasse, S.C.; Cuisinarts, Inc., Greenwich, Conn.; KitchenAid, Inc., Troy, Ohio; Oster, Milwaukee, Wis.